We'll Support You Evermore
Rugby League fans' memories

Dean Bell in action for Wigan at Central Park
(Photo: Andrew Cudbertson)

David Kuzio

LONDON LEAGUE PUBL1

We'll Support You Evermore
Rugby League fans' memories

A CIP catalogue record for this book is available from the British Library.

First published in Great Britain in May 2006 by:
London League Publications Ltd, P.O. Box 10441, London E14 8WR

ISBN: 1-903659-26-4

Cover design by: Stephen McCarthy Graphic Design
                               46, Clarence Road, London N15 5BB

Layout: Peter Lush

Printed and bound by: Biddles Ltd
                        King's Lynn, Norfolk, Great Britain

**This book is dedicated to my son Ryan Adam
and my late daughter Kate xxxxx**

Foreword

I first started playing rugby league when I was aged seven. Because I am a Widnes lad I started to go and watch them, and at that time Widnes were the most successful side.

Being from Widnes all my friends were into rugby, it was like a natural progression and with me being a big lad it was fairly obvious I would play rugby.

My first club was at Cronton in Widnes, I stayed there until I went to Widnes Tigers before signing professional at Salford.

I think playing rugby was more of a social thing at that age because all of my friends played and we would all meet up. I was lucky enough at the age of 11 to play in a curtain raiser for the challenge cup final at Wembley.

That was when I knew at the age of 11 I wanted to play rugby league as a career. In that cup final in 1983, Featherstone Rovers beat Hull 14-12. It was a major honour to play in that curtain raiser.

I was lucky enough that I actually played quite well on the day and the scouts started to show an interest and began coming to watch my amateur games. I tell everyone that rugby league is all about luck, I was lucky to get signed professional but there were loads of great players about then that never got signed, and they just eventually fell to the wayside. It's just about being in the right place at the right time.

Looking back at my years in the game I think if I wasn't playing professionally I would still be playing the game on a Saturday afternoon, and I probably wouldn't have a badly broken nose and all my other injuries. As everyone knows, I was a good looking lad before I started getting all the knocks to the head.

I know I was lucky enough to have had 10 years at Wigan where it is a quite demanding club, the pressure is on everyone because we all want to win things. Most times it can be really good but it can also be very hard, but at the end of the day I am no better than the next bloke in any job just because I am good with a ball.

I have a lot of memories through playing rugby league, I will always remember that curtain raiser at the age of 11. When I was 17 I was banned from playing the game for a year so I suppose you could say I will never forget that.

I will always remember playing under Steve O'Neill at Salford that was a memorable time for me when I first signed for the reserves. You could say we weren't the most successful side but the team spirit was tremendous and my first involvement of being in a winning team.

When I signed for Wigan my first memory was winning my first trophy which was the Regal Trophy. We had beaten St Helens and Joe Lydon came up to me after the game and handed me the match ball, he said: "Well played kid, here is something you will appreciate when you look back on it."

At the time I didn't think much of it, but now I do, I suppose the old fossil was right. It was a really nice gesture, and the kind of thing I would do now for a youngster if we won a trophy. Its small things like having a match ball that make you enjoy your memories.

Steve O'Neill once said something to me years ago which I will never ever forget: "Always remember the people you meet on your way up because you'll see them first on your way down."

I have mentioned some of my earlier memories and I suppose they can be classed as my fondest in rugby league, but captaining Ireland in the World Cup has to be my proudest moment. I have been capped 15 times for Great Britain but the best moment had to be leading out Ireland it was a fantastic honour for me.

Seeing as this is a book about the fans I feel I need to explain to you all what the fans mean to me.

Speccies mean the world to me and I can honestly say that. I will always have time for the fans, and I will always go and clap them at the end of the game. Sometimes after a defeat it is extremely hard to pick yourself up and clap because all the players want to do is go home.

I can honestly say I don't know any player who intentionally goes out to lose a game, we all go out to win and when we are losing and the fans get on the players back it can be a bit difficult to pick yourselves up after being in a rut, but we go out and try and I know it hurts the fans like it hurts us when we lose.

I'm not best pleased with players who don't have time for the fans because at the end of the day it's the speccies that make or break a club. If you look at the top five clubs in Super League, they have a large fan base who go watching week in week out, and they are the heart of any club.

I am being truthful here when I say I have all the time in the world for the Wigan fans, they were fantastic to me in my 10 years and I will always spend a few minutes talking to them. Because some fans live for rugby, they work all week just waiting for the next game, so the least we can do is take a few minutes to appreciate them.

Terry O'Connor
September 2004.

Introduction

Dignity, respect and humility are words which can best be used to describe both the players' and the fans' emotions and attitudes towards the game of rugby league and towards each other.

For evidence, one has to look no further than the club bar or sponsors lounge after each match, where even heroes of the calibre of Andy Farrell, Paul Sculthorpe, Danny McGuire and company rub shoulders with their supporters and form an orderly queue behind them before buying their drinks.

Here is a sport which still affords its star players the dignity and respect they deserve, but expects them to display the humility which never takes them too far away from the local community and which never keeps them behind closed doors, hidden away from the presence of the public by burly security guards, and also never massages their egos sufficiently to give them delusions as to their self importance.

Rugby league players and their fans have never lost sight of the fact that they are a part of the local community and are representatives of that community. Unlike other sports they are at one and in an age of hype, media, spin and sham celebrity status, our players and our game are looked upon as examples of the honesty and integrity which many others have now lost.

At the age of five years I could sit on the wall or rickety wooden fence at the side of the entrance to the pitch at Knowsley Road and pat my heroes on the back as they ran to do battle with the opposition. After the game I could offer them my tattered autograph book in the tiny tea room and never once would it be refused. Today I can still pat a player on the back in the dressing room after the most intense of contests and later enjoy a pint and a chat with him in the lounge bar, as can other supporters.

Rugby league players can be regularly in the newspapers and on television, and many of its leading players may be well known via the backing of some of the biggest names in the business world, also the XIII-a-side code may also now be forced to cope with finances undreamed of in any previous decade, but the game, its players and its fans have never lost their respect for each other and their identity in the community.

That's why having enjoyed the sport as a fan, a player, a journalist, and a commentator for over 60 years, rugby league is still so attractive to me and so much a part of my life.

I hope that everyone can keep enjoying our great game.

Ray French
December 2004.

Acknowledgements

I would like to acknowledge the following people who have helped make my dream of writing a book come true.

Firstly I would like to thank my loving fiancée Christine, who without her support and guidance I wouldn't have completed this project. She has had to put up with my bad moods and writer's block over the past year or so. Also to my mum Kathleen, dad Adam, sister Karen and mother in law to be Margaret, without their help and encouragement I would have given up ages ago.

Peter Lush and Dave Farrar from London League Publications Ltd have been very helpful and encouraging with my quest to publish this book, and they saw potential in the subject when I sent them a rough draft. So I thank them for their help.

Ray French is a very busy man, but he still had time to write a few words on rugby league, having him in this book is a great honour.

During his final year at Wigan, I became quite friendly with Terry O'Connor and after helping with his testimonial year he agreed to put together a few words on what it is like to be a professional rugby league player and what the fans mean to him. Many thanks to Terry for his contribution.

Michael O'Hare sub-edited the book; Andrew Cudbertson, Robert Gate and Peter Lush supplied photos, Steve McCarthy designed the cover and Peter Lush did the layout. Thank you to all of them.

Finally, everyone who took the time and effort to reply to my e-mails on Rlfans.com and letters in *League Express* and *League Weekly*, without your memories this book would still be a pipe dream. You have all been awarded your few minutes of fame and have all received a mention.

I started off wanting to thank the fans of rugby league with a book dedicated to them about them, and I think I have managed that. So with that I thank you.

You really are the greatest spectators in the world.

David Kuzio
March 2006

About the author

David Kuzio has been following rugby league for over 20 years with Wigan. He is an NCTJ qualified journalist who spent three years at the *Wigan Evening Post* before joining Press Association as a sports journalist with Teletext. He played rugby league for Ashton Bears for 10 years, usually at hooker or scrum-half, and was in the starting XIII for their first ever game against Orrell St James.

This is his first book. An account of his memories of rugby league appears in Chapter 16.

Contents

In the text, the author's comments are in *italic*, the contributions to the book are in standard print.

Halifax fans protest against club amalgamations and the proposed
introduction of Super League – April 1995 (Photo: Robert Gate)

London Broncos fans celebrate a try at The Valley.
(Photo: Peter Lush)

1. Hooked on Rugby League

The majority of rugby league fans will have a team they have supported since childhood, but there are some who don't follow one specific club and just attend as many matches as possible – all for the love of rugby league.

This chapter has contributions from these fans, but starts with two people who have been involved in professional rugby league at the top level.

The man in the middle

Former Grade 1 referee David Asquith has seen and refereed many games of rugby league and has had to make some very important calls as an official and video referee.

As a teenager I was sports mad, particularly football and rugby league. I followed Leeds United in the Don Revie days. And when Leeds were playing away I used to watch the odd Batley game.

Once I passed my driving test I realised I could watch Batley home and away. This continued into my married life, watching Batley home and away even though I lived in Durham. One season I only missed five matches. Was this dedication or madness?

Then, after moving to Bradford, I became one of the biggest critics of referees, thinking I could do better than the pratt in black.

So I got involved with refereeing, starting refereeing amateur matches in the Pennine League and then the Yorkshire League after moving to York.

It took me 10 years to move up the grades to the top flight of Grade 1. Over the next eight years I refereed 170 first team matches, including numerous games on television. I also refereed a student international in France.

Then after the first summer season in 1996 I had to give up refereeing at the top level due to a knee injury. I thought the world had collapsed around me. Greg McCallum, who was then the referees' supremo, moved me to the assessing and video referee panel. Over the next couple of seasons I was the first video referee at an international at Wembley, Great

Britain versus Australia, the first video referee at a Grand Final at Old Trafford in 1998, and the first video referee at a Challenge Cup Final in 1999, the last one to be played at Wembley. I also coached the Grade 2 referees for a couple of seasons.

Now, 26 years after refereeing my first match I am still turning out on a Saturday afternoon refereeing matches in the Yorkshire League and I have no signs of stopping. Last February I refereed my 1,000th match. I am still on the RFL's assessing panel out covering matches every Sunday in the summer.

During the last 26 years I have had thousands of happy, nervous, and sometimes sad experiences. I have made a lot of friends who will be with me lifelong. Referees are a strange, but fantastic breed who have a tremendous sense of humour. I have lots of wonderful memories along with the record of seeing every Challenge Cup Final since 1965.

My interest and love of the greatest game never tires.

John Etty is a former professional rugby league player having successful stints at Batley, Oldham and Wakefield Trinity, Yorkshire, England and the British Empire XIII, between 1944 and 1961.

Any fan of Oldham will remember his name. He was elected into the club's Hall of Fame in 1995. John recalls his early days in the game.

Playing the game

In 1935, when I was a schoolboy aged 8, I climbed an oak tree in Batley's Wilton Park to collect acorns. The park ranger appeared shaking his stick. I ran off and escaped. Later in life I met him again and we laughed about the incident.

The park ranger was Jim Gath who played for the Batley rugby league side as a forward in the 1897 Challenge Cup Final – the very first - when Batley defeated St Helens 10-3. When I met Jim for the second time I was captain of Batley RLFC.

At the age of 10 I bought my first pair of football boots from a shoe shop in Batley, the lady who sold me my boots was the mother-in-law of former rugby league referee, Derek Brown.

2

Around that time I became a mascot of an amateur rugby league side based at the Coach and Six pub in Batley, my late father John 'Jack' Etty ran the team, which reached two local cup finals.

In 1943 I played my first game of rugby league for an unofficial seven-a-side team in a local competition at Mount Pleasant. I managed to score our team's try after a long sprint, although we lost the game 10-5 to Dewsbury Wheelwright Grammar School.

I played amateur rugby league for Dewsbury YMCA at 17, helping the team to win the Championship and Challenge Cup in the Leeds under-18 league. I then turned professional and gained every winners medal possible in seven competitions.

Over the years I have enjoyed playing the game as a professional and I still enjoy matches as a spectator.

Andy Gilderdale writes about what rugby league means to him.

So, what's so special about rugby league then?

So what makes rugby league such a special game for me? Well, the sport has a history like something out of a Victorian soap opera. The down-trodden, working class northerners broke away from the Rugby Football Union to form a league of their own.

A league where the working man would be entitled to compensation for the wages he lost playing the game he loved. This led to 100 years of bigotry and oppression, as the 'establishment' union game sought to hold down the young upstart, denying it players, facilities and publicity, and reinforcing the image of the cloth cap against the bowler hat.

The game itself is the closest thing to gladiatorial combat since the Romans decided that Lions versus Christians just wasn't selling tickets like it used to. There are speed, power, athleticism - all combined with twinkling feet and a sleight of hand worthy of the Royal Ballet and the Magic Circle.

It is a game where even the unlikeliest men can go on to become heroes and legends. Brian Bevan, a wiry, chain-smoking Australian who looked as far from a professional athlete as you could probably hope to see stands alone as the greatest try-scorer in the history of the game. It is a game where the good little 'uns – Jonty Parkin, Alex Murphy, Roger Millward and Andy Gregory - can compete on an even footing with, and sometimes embarrass, their bigger adversaries - giants of men such as Ken Gee, Arthur Clues, Jim Mills and Joe Vagana.

Then let's throw the fans into the equation. League fans are a breed apart, perfectly balanced with a chip on either shoulder. A body of thousands, all capable of shouting the word: "Forward!" at exactly the same time, as if telepathically controlled. Yet some of the humour you'll find on league terraces - or more commonly these days in the seats, as clubs move towards better facilities and more modern stadia - is unique at sporting events. There is no need for football style segregation here; banter is rife without extending into brawling. Fans meet and mingle before, during and after games without requiring the riot squad on standby.

As a kid growing up in the 1970s, football grounds to me were places of hate, of violence and an ugly atmosphere far removed from that I experienced on the terraces at Headingley.

That's what makes this game so special to me, and to millions like myself, all around the globe from Pontefract to Papua New Guinea, Clitheroe to Carcassonne or Anlaby to Auckland. It's truly a game of the people, by the people and for the people.

Paddy Kane explains how he started following rugby league.

I was born and bred in Cumbria, so I have always been around rugby league. However, it was only when I went to university in Derby, aged 18, that I started to watch the game.

Through access to Sky Sports in the common room of my university halls of residence, I followed the progress of Paris St Germain in Super League I in 1996 and was hooked for life. I found the coverage very exciting and the no-nonsense humour of commentators Eddie and Stevo was hilarious.

My interest in football gradually died and I will always remember my first live game at Central Park, Wigan when they played the Hunter Mariners in the World Club Challenge.

The atmosphere was first class and I loved the banter of the fans, not like the aggressiveness and intimidation you get in football.

I think the saddest moment was the demise of Paris, it was such a step backwards for the game and I couldn't help feeling very angry that we, as a sport, had shot ourselves in the foot.

Since university, I have managed to convert several friends, one of them went on to form a new rugby league club in Lancaster. I now organise a works touch rugby league team and still like to spread the word on the greatest game wherever possible.

Through my job as a banker, I have since been exiled in the Isle of Man and Jersey. Despite my living arrangements I still manage to get to the occasional Super League game and every year, of course, the Challenge Cup Final and Super League Grand Final.

Frank Williamson has followed rugby league for 25 years and his love for the game still runs strong.

I got hooked on rugby league in the mid-1980s although I live in Durham.

At that time I spent Saturday afternoons wandering around shops and felt sure that there was more to life than that. So I went a couple of times to watch Middlesbrough play football and almost fell asleep in the process. In 1987, in desperation I took my wife for a day out to Manchester and went to Wigan, to watch Leigh play St Helens, in a Challenge Cup semi-final. After that game I was hooked.

I had watched rugby league before in the Billy Boston era at Central Park and at Station Road, when I was living in Manchester for a short while and had loved the atmosphere then, so I suppose that I was not surprised to be captivated by it again.

Living in Durham, I am not attached to any one team but over the years I have variously followed Leeds, Castleford, York and now, surprisingly, the London Broncos, because I

5

visit London quite regularly. But essentially I am a follower of the game itself.

The three most memorable games I have seen over the years all involve defeats of Wigan, not because I have anything against Wigan, but because they were such a great team at the time and for anyone to beat them required a great performance, which always lead to a super game.

The first of these was on 7 October 1990, it was my first visit to the Boulevard and my first experience of the wonderful singing coming from the Threepenny Stand.

The next was at Headingley on 11 December 1994, when I was chuffed when I realised fact that I did not need a programme - I knew every player on the pitch.

Finally, I was at the wonderful game at Tynecastle, Edinburgh, on 1 August 1999 when Gateshead Thunder beat Wigan - I was hoarse when I left the ground. Wonderful memories, and I am sure there are many more to come.

Dominic Hornsby is a rugby league mad publican in Merseyside, but was brought up in one of the heartlands of rugby league – Whitehaven.

Now living in Liverpool, happily married and the licensee of a very successful public house, I am a true rugby league man.

I am Whitehaven born and bred and I truly believe 'The Greatest Game of All' is the best sport in the world. Having played the game at amateur level and also having watched and been involved with it for the past 20 years, I am still in awe at the sheer excitement it brings. From the elite athletes on the pitch, to the tremendous atmosphere at every ground, through to the passion of the people, the heritage and very proud history of the game – I love it.

Memories of all kinds of occasions spring to mind, my first ever visit to the Recreation Ground – the home of Whitehaven RLFC - to my first experience of a test match – the Great Britain versus Australia second test of the 1986 Ashes series at Elland Road, Challenge Cup Finals, Super League Grand Finals and my first images of State of Origin, plus meeting players like Alex Murphy, Paul Sculthorpe and Andy Gregory over the years. All are fantastic memories.

My dad introduced me to Alex Murphy after the test match in 1986 outside Elland Road and I got his autograph. My dad told my brother and me: "You have just shaken hands with one of the greatest ever players."

One of the most nail-biting games I ever saw was at Old Trafford in 1990. This was the second test against Australia when Mal Meninga broke our hearts in injury time. The loudest roar I ever heard at a rugby league match was also at Old Trafford, at the second test in 1994 when Phil Clarke led out the Great Britain team. Mistakenly, I really thought we were going to win the Ashes.

One of the best tries I ever saw was Joe Lydon's for Great Britain in the first test at Old Trafford against the Australians in 1986 – it was electrifying. But my favourite ground has to be Headingley, I was there one day when Leeds beat Wigan, it was the early 1990s and Ellery Hanley was the Leeds captain and there were around 25,000 spectators – it was a wonderful occasion.

We need to protect our game and also honour our heroes. Players over the years who deserve recognition include Wagstaff, Bevan, Boston, Murphy, Prescott, Whitely, Turner, Huddart, Karalius, Gasnier, Raper, Sterling, Kenny, Lewis, Meninga, Miles, Schofield, Lydon, Hanley, Farrell, Edwards, Sculthorpe, McGuire and Morley. In fact the list is endless.

I respect every player who takes to the field in what is the toughest sport on Earth and the thrills they give us are unparalleled in any other sport in the world.

I love the game so much that I almost eat and breathe it – when I was at school my mum used to say: "If you put as much time and energy into your studies as your rugby, you'll be a genius." I have a huge video collection and once even knew the commentary of every one off by heart – I thought I was Ray French.

Tom Dorcey reveals his favourite memories of rugby league. Although he is a Huddersfield fan he loves to attend as many games as possible.

I was taught to play rugby union at school. We call it the rah-rah way or kick and push as they used to say in Huddersfield, but I spent half my pocket money on a weekly special from

Skipton to Keighley's Lawkholme Lane, a shilling round trip plus entrance fee - where I once saw Bert Cook drop a goal from the touchline just inside his own half in the early 1950s.

After that great kick, my second fondest memory of 'the greatest game of all' was helping to clear the snow off the pitch at Fartown in the early 1950s. My reward was free entrance into the match to watch the team of all stars, Lionel Cooper, Pat Devery, Johnny Hunter and the late, great Billy Banks who became a great mate of mine many years later. Watching players like that was well worth freezing your bits off, it was an absolute privilege.

Another memory that seems to be imprinted in my mind is the 1970 Championship Final: Bradford Northern versus Widnes at Station Road, Swinton. Bradford won the game and after the match I cadged a lift from a fellow Fartowner back over the Pennines into civilisation in the back of a mini-van.

In the car park at Station Road after the club had closed we saw Ian van Bellen and Neil Fox wandering about looking for the Bradford bus, which had gone. These two big lads were stranded and wanted a lift back with us, which we had to refuse.

Later I learned they'd got a taxi home and booked it in the name of the club and the Bradford secretary went bananas, Yorkshire men penny pinching as usual.

My last, but not least, memory of a lifetime of joy was at a St Helens versus Dewsbury match. There was a slight altercation between Trevor 'the tank' Walker and John Warlow, when a middle-aged lady ran on to the pitch and started to attack the former. Was this the first incident of televised crowd trouble?

It turned out she was John Warlow's landlady and perhaps she was worried she would not receive next month's rent.

Ian Gourlay from Hamilton in Scotland explains why he decided to follow the XIII-a-side game, when football and rugby union are the number one sports in his country.

Way back in the black-and-white, Eddie Waring days of the 1960s, I saw rugby league on television. Here in West Central Scotland, football was the game and only the toffs or would-be toffs had anything to do with rugby – and the 'rugby' was union.

Like my peers I was a football fan, supporting my local club, Hamilton Academicals (the Accies) as a third-generation supporter – with my family having followed them since their foundation.

In the 1960s, even without any knowledge of rugby league, I said that if the game had been played in Scotland I would have watched it. I had arguments with rah-rah colleagues who extolled the virtues of the 'amateur' game over the 'professional' game and ran down league at every opportunity. Having virtually no knowledge of the intricacies of either code, I could not put up a great argument, but was not in anyway convinced that union was the better game.

In the late 1980s I became so disenchanted with football that I virtually gave up on the game (and this at a time when the Accies were having their best spell in my lifetime). The game itself had become so predictable and boring and was so far removed from the one I had played as a boy, it had become unrecognisable. I wanted an alternative and rugby league was the obvious choice.

I wrote to the Rugby Football League requesting information and received a very pleasant reply together with a huge supply of literature concerning the game, ranging from a copy of the rules to an edition of the contemporary leading magazine *Open Rugby*.

Here was a whole new world of sport. I read the literature and was to discover that, having been taught the rules of football in early adolescence, I knew them quite well, but learning the rules of rugby league was as difficult as an academic exercise. However, my wife and I stuck with it and soon had a working knowledge of the laws of the game.

We were also speedway fans in the 1970s, and back then we once had to phone Workington's Derwent Park to check the time of a meeting. We were advised by the person who answered to come early, because before the speedway meeting there would be a rugby league game in the afternoon. This we did, and that game between Workington Town and Blackpool Borough was the first live league game we witnessed. I don't remember the score, but it was a big win for Town.

However, our serious interest started in about 1988. We could travel to Carlisle, Workington and Whitehaven and back in a day. Any further would require an overnight stay. We did however, attend the Premiership Finals at Old Trafford from about 1989 until they ended – sadly, in my view, the Grand Final is nowhere near as good an event.

As far as supporting a team is concerned – and this won't please the editor, we always had a soft spot for St Helens, not because they were one of the leading clubs, but because in the aforementioned black and white television days, they were the only team we could always recognise with their dark V on a white background.

Because Wigan played in the same strip as the Accies – red (cherry really for Wigan) and white hoops, I did lean towards them too, but as our interest and knowledge of the game grew, we went more to the Saints – and I need hardly say that consequently our liking for Wigan diminished.

A few years back I sent a letter to the *Wakefield Express* condemning the deduction of points for Wakefield Trinity for salary cap infringement. I pointed out a similar situation had arisen with the Accies, only in their case the points deduction had meant relegation. I received a letter from a member of their supporters club thanking me for my support. My wife and I subsequently visited Wakefield, more in solidarity than anything else, and we were treated very well. We are still in touch with the Wakefield fans.

We only see two or three live games each season for reasons of cost and time, but we try to take in two games in one visit whenever we can – Castleford on a Saturday night, and Wakefield on a Sunday afternoon. St Helens is easily reached from the M6. However, I have never been a driver and my wife has arthritis so all our trips now are by train.

We have never regretted our involvement with league and always enjoy our trips to England for the games. We have recently made contact with a young Saints fan who we met at Saints versus Huddersfield in 2004 on our annual trip to Knowsley Road who keeps us up to date with events at the club.

2. Barrow Raiders

Peter Knibbs has been watching Barrow for over 28 years and is confident his passion for the club will never die. Here he recalls the moments that made him fall in love with the club.

It is not surprising that I am a Barrow rugby league supporter.

I am 48 years old and my earliest memory is of my grandad, who went to school with the great Barrow player Willie Horne, telling me tales of playing rugby on some open land near his home in Barrow with Willie and others.

My earliest recollection of Craven Park is watching Bill Burgess, Tommy Dawes, Harry Hughes, Tom Brophy, Keith Jarrett and many more in the 1960s.

I remember listening on the radio to the 1967 Challenge Cup Final between Barrow and Featherstone Rovers. We lost 17-12.

Two of my greatest memories however, are actually from the 1980s. One is beating Hull 13-10 at a snowy Headingley in the John Player Cup semi-final in January 1981, and, until 2004, when we won National League 2, the last trophy win in Barrow's history was, of course, beating Widnes 12-8 in the 1983 Lancashire Cup Final at Central Park, Wigan, now sadly no more.

I have been a season ticket holder at Barrow every year for the last 28 years and now my nine-year-old daughter is also a season ticket holder.

People say to me that I am daft to go to the rugby so regularly but I, like many others in the land, love my club and my rugby league.

Bradford Northern versus Halifax in April 1966. Ronnie James running with the ball for Halifax. (Photo: Courtesy Robert Gate)

John Etty in action for
Wakefield Trinity
(Photo: Courtesy Robert Gate)

3. Bradford Bulls

Harold Winterburn has almost 60 years of watching rugby league at Odsal.

It was 1947 when I first seriously began following rugby league, after a few years of watching rugby union. My older brothers took me to Odsal. Over the years, I have enjoyed each visit.

I have witnessed good teams, bad teams and during one difficult time in the 1960s, no teams at all. At Odsal you do feel you are a long distance from the pitch when standing behind the posts but you have to admit it is still a clear view, unlike the obstructions you get at most grounds.

We have of course been promised a Super-Dome, but Bradford seemed to miss the boat on that one.

The great players I've seen would fill a book, but for me one Bradford star stood way out on his own – he was Ernest Ward, whose class for Great Britain and Northern was there to be seen week-in, week-out.

The updated Bulls have given the supporters 10 good years in Super League and overall rugby league in general has improved, with its fast flowing football.

Bradford Bulls fan Sam Grundy recalls his introduction to the game.

No more boring Sundays

To those people uninitiated into the world of rugby league Sunday afternoons in winter are renowned for being the dullest days of the year. Nowadays little has changed, but back in 1986 they were to me the most boring days of the week.

As a 13-year-old I had little interest in much of what was on offer on a wet Sunday in October. The usual thing that happened was that I spent the day with my dad and we went around the many attractions of the Bradford district. I had been doing this since the age of six and by the age of 13 I now knew more about the contents of Cartwright Hall Art Gallery and Cliffe Castle in Keighley than their respective curators. Sundays were usually a day spent going to museums or the pictures and then a visit to relatives for tea. What Sunday would be complete without an episode of *Bullseye*, then in its heyday, or *Highway* with Harry Secombe warbling away in the background? A day of excitement it was not. However that was soon to change and soon Sundays would be the most eagerly awaited day of the week.

One October Sunday my dad announced that we were "going to the rugby". This initially didn't fill me with that much excitement being the typical easily bored teenager. My dad had played union when I was a little kid and I wasn't struck with it but I was willing to give it a go. When he said we were going to Leeds to see Bradford Northern play I was a bit more interested, it wasn't going to be type of rugby I had previously known that involved 30 rotund men playing "pile on" in front of a handful of people and a dog.

Arriving at Headingley that day opened my eyes. The crowd was around 7,514, small by today's standards but to an impressionable 13-year-old it was *huge*. After a quick explanation of the rules the match was underway. The game was totally absorbing, there never seemed to be a dull moment and I was completely carried away with it. At half-time we changed ends and walked behind the main stand to the eastern terrace with the Bradford fans. I felt part of something good.

For some reason there was never any doubt which team I should be supporting. My dad was from Bradford, we were stood with the Bradford fans and I happened to be born in Bradford. That said I'd been brought up in Pudsey which although it is proud of its status as a town on its own is more Leeds-centric. Throughout my life so far all my friends seemed to be Leeds fans of some description. It was "Leeds this" and "Leeds that" for as long as I could remember. Here was my chance to claim a team as my own.

It helped that Bradford Northern were the better team that day. They ran out winners 12-4 thanks to a super try by Welsh scrum-half Terry Holmes. Leeds provided a suitable pantomime villain in Kevin Rayne - or was it Keith? My memory is a bit hazy now.

Anyway, upon the final whistle I was hooked and eager for more. I sought out the fixtures for the following week and

14

announced to my dad that we were "going to the rugby" again next week to see Northern take on Featherstone at Odsal. The Rugby League bug had bitten me and I was now a fan for life. *Bullseye* and Harry Secombe's warbling were now a thing of the past. Thanks dad.

Michael Farren reflects on a lifetime following Bradford, both Northern and Bulls.

A constant presence in my life

I never had much choice about being a Bradford Northern supporter. From the cradle, my dad bombarded me with geographical, ideological and mythological reasons to back the team. The first two – that it was my local and my class-based heritage – were compelling enough, but I believe it was the mythology that clinched it. Ernest Ward, Frank Whitcombe, Trevor Foster, Jack McLean, Joe Philips... these were the principal deities, and I drank in the tales of their legendary exploits as the child of a clergyman might rejoice in Bible stories.

Dad started taking me to Odsal around the age of three and I had my first season ticket (costing two shillings and sixpence) shortly after. As a result, I don't have a first rugby league memory – just a constant presence in my life that gradually solidified into actual matches, actual players and actual stadia. That presence was woven ever more tightly into the fabric of my life by neighbours who were equally enthusiastic about the team (and who, 40 years later, remain my match day companions), and by the regular visits of Percy Pitts, the local mobile greengrocer, who was fanatical about rugby league, and two of whose sons later played for the club.

The memories I do have from that era tend toward the Proustian: the taste of oxtail soup or flask coffee with rum; the smell of a certain type of pipe tobacco; the sensation of being lifted over a turnstile; the feeling of getting home to remove frozen feet from two sets of socks and fleece-lined boots. However, individual names started to stick in my mind – David Stockwell, David Hill, Bak Diabira, Terry Price... They existed in an eternal present of childhood perception, and I could not begin to imagine a team without them.

Events start to come into focus for me with the Challenge Cup run that took us to Wembley in 1973. I remember the huge crowd at Odsal for our unexpected defeat of Wigan. I remember celebrating our equally unexpected semi-final defeat of Dewsbury's team of stars (including my own future heroes Jeff Grayshon and Nigel Stephenson), by going onto the Headingley pitch and sprinting the length of the touchline to ground my rolled-up cagoule under the posts.

The trip to Wembley was a fog, swirling around islands of clear recollection. It was my first time in London. The Underground posters for *This Sporting Life* director Lindsay Anderson's then current film *O Lucky Man* seemed cruelly mocking after the final whistle. It was my first time in a such an enormous crowd; being obliged to sing *Nice One, Cyril* seemed ominously prophetic of Cyril Kellett's record-breaking goal kicking performance. It was my first time at a major final, and an effective introduction to the next 20-odd years of under-achievement. Featherstone centre Mick Smith's weekly re-enactment of his spectacular humiliation of the Bradford defence at the start of *Grandstand* throughout most of that period only hammered the point home.

If the Wembley run marked the beginning of the historical era, it was the following year that made it my era, in the same way as the '50's had been my father's. When our star goal kicker, Eddie Tees, abruptly and permanently quit rugby league, there were some worries that it would disrupt our efforts to get promotion from the second division. Even though our next match was against Doncaster, then the whipping boys of rugby league, there was further concern about an untried 16-year-old taking over Tees' role. When Keith Mumby seized the opportunity by scoring 12 tries and a goal, there was a new divinity to add to those of my dad. Keith, though, was someone I could identify with – just a few years older than me and living close enough that I'd bump into him at the newsagent's. He was my addition to the pantheon, in the same way that I was adding LPs by Bowie and Dylan to my dad's Glenn Miller and Ella Fitzgerald. Dad, however, accepted Keith somewhat more readily.

I went on to revel in the success and character (Ian 'Selwyn' Van Bellen and 'bionic' Jack Austin anyone?) of the Peter Fox team, culminating in David Barends' spectacular dive to score the clinching try against Widnes in the Play Off final at the much missed Station Road, Swinton. However, when I went to university, the fact that I could no longer attend matches every week meant that my relationship with the club and the sport altered subtly – much as I clung to both as badges of identity when surrounded by aesthetes and southerners, for whom rugby league was synonymous with barbarism.

I almost drifted away from the game over the next few years, due to work, relationships and geography, but supporting Northern had been too much of an investment by me and my dad for us to allow it to lapse altogether. Having a sympathetic partner and moving back to the area allowed me get back into the Odsal habit just before Super League kicked in.

With the advent of Super League, I accepted that the era I considered my own had effectively passed, but I was pleased with the crowds of newcomers enjoying the game. I also enjoyed the success, which I felt I'd earned in those years of under achievement, and the exoticism – "Did you ever think you'd be cheering someone called 'Shontayne'?" I asked my dad. I hope the game and the Bulls will give as much pleasure and as much of a sense of identity and pride to the new generation.

Barrow legend Phil Jackson scoring at Wembley for Barrow in the
1957 Challenge Cup Final. Barrow lost 9-7 to Leeds.
(Photo: Courtesy Keith Nutter)

Bradford Bulls' mascot Bullman
– symbol of much of their
success in Super League – at
Odsal in 2000.
(Photo: Peter Lush)

4. Bramley Buffaloes

Bramley club president Cliff Spracklen outlines what it is like being a Bramley fan. Deciding on supporting the underdogs turned into a real family affair and he backed his son Lee 100 per cent when he fought to get Bramley back into the rugby league community after the club unexpectedly folded in 1999.

It is often said that the fans make a team, and in Bramley's case, this is certainly true.

"Supporting the dream or just plain awkward?" - One fan's support for Bramley

Although I had been to rugby league matches throughout my childhood, which meant, in Leeds, going to watch Hunslet, Bramley and Leeds in roughly equal proportions, I did not make a fundamental decision about who I supported until the day of the 1957 Challenge Cup Final.

Rugby league was my sport because that was the only game played at school, the then Burmantofts C of E Primary School. The one famous rugby league son of Burmantofts was future Leeds and Great Britain international Graham Eccles, and he is the only star I can remember playing in the same team as, even though he was a year or two younger than the rest of us.

But professional careers were not the aim. It was something you did for enjoyment. It was just natural to support the game, particularly when teachers organised the occasional trip to a professional match. Brought up in East Leeds all three clubs could claim my support, and in those days ease of getting to the ground by bus was a dominant factor. Ironically this put Leeds into third place, even though as the crow flies Headingley was slightly nearer than Hunslet's Parkside or Bramley's Barley Mow.

What did it for me was, I suppose, my belligerent attitude. On the train chartered by the Leeds and Hunslet Schools Rugby League for the trip to London, for the Final, I was overwhelmed by Leeds fans almost to a man, or boy, decked out in the blue and amber rosettes of Leeds. I might have been 11 years old, but I had decided then that I was not going to be one of the crowd. So for the three hours it took to reach London I must have been a pain in the proverbial as I argued with anybody and everybody that Barrow were going to hammer the Loiners out of sight. Even being proved wrong by a Leeds win in what was a very close game, noted for the kicking duel between the opposing full-backs I swore unreservedly that Leeds were jammy and that Barrow should have won.

As if to justify it I won five shillings (25p) in the *Yorkshire Evening News* competition asking kids to write a match report. Leeds must have been lucky. It said so in my report.

After that and my arrival at grammar school, where most of the pupils came from north of the river, and if they were not rugby union types they supported the Loiners, my allegiances were confirmed. That is confirmed in the sense that I was not a Leeds fan, but had a strong feeling for both Hunslet and Bramley, who I had rationalised by then were both underdogs and working class. The fact that many engineers, printers and clothing workers on Kirkstall Road supported Leeds was not allowed to alter this fundamental fact of life. In any case supporting the underdog used to be a fine English tradition, only withering these days as television fans are becoming as likely to support the big, overexposed so-called glamour clubs like Manchester United in football, or Bradford Bulls in rugby league.

But in those days Leeds had the pedigree history with lots of trophies, bigger crowds and a bigger stadium. But they never had shirts to match the amber and black of Bramley, nor the myrtle, white and flame of Hunslet. Not that replica shirts were available in those days, only the very unimaginative rosettes, which look so dated today.

In those days people were less mobile, most did not have cars or television, so most people just supported their local club. Playing football at grammar school I also supported Leeds United. But then many fans supported both codes, though I never knew anyone who supported rugby union, which was quite clearly the game for toffs. There were no commuters so people lived, worked and played in their local communities. At that time too all three rugby league clubs in Leeds could command healthy gates. Leeds United were an average and poorly supported second division side, with Hunslet averaging more than 7,000 in the Second Division even as late as 1962, and Bramley capable of regularly pulling in up to 4,000 even after the post-war attendance boom had declined.

I admit to originally being a Hunslet fan and, to be honest they had some good sides, regularly contributing players to the Great Britain team and appearing in a classic Championship Final against St Helens in 1959. My involvement with the famous Hunslet Boys Club in later years also brought me into contact with the Hunslet rugby league club, to the point where I arranged trips to France for them alongside Hunslet Boys Club teams.

But Bramley had the Barley Mow. What a name. I didn't quite know what that represented but it sounded exotic: fields of ripe barley willowing in the summer sun in an English idyll.

Well it was idyllic even if it had a creaking stand and was so often a quagmire, churned up by what seemed to be to be a pack of giants. But the Barley Mow was exotic to a youngster. That exotica came in the shape of the first Maori I had ever seen. I remember one day my dad saying: "Let's go to Bramley, they've got a Maori at full-back." We lived in Burmantofts then and it meant a bus ride. Having served in the army in North Africa alongside Indian and Anzac soldiers my dad would tell me about the different people he had met Ghurkhas, Sikhs, Aussies and Maoris. Burmantofts was then mainly white, though with a large Italian and Irish population. He had taken me to Parkside to see an Australian, the legendary Arthur Clues. "Tough buggers the Aussies were," he said, and Clues fitted the bill perfectly, forever involved in a ruckus. I remember getting my first new boots from Arthur Clues's sports shop in Leeds. As to the Maoris, they were "very proud people, and they perform a war dance" he said. I was intrigued. I had never seen a Maori. I wanted to see a Maori 'war dance', or Haka, as we now know it.

So we went to the Barley Mow. I saw Maori full-back Johnny Wilson for the first time. Though disappointed at not seeing him perform the Haka, I was amazed at the man himself. Broad-shouldered, with big hands, like shovels, nothing got past him. It seems odd to say a full-back dominated the game, but Johnny Wilson did just that, his marksmanship with the boot being an additional bonus. Wilson was a true Bramley stalwart, later taking over as landlord of the closely associated Barley Mow pub, before continuing as a popular pub landlord in Leeds until he died a few years ago. He was a proud Maori, Bramley legend and a wonderful man. He was reason enough to support any team.

It was appropriate that he played on the ground that had staged the first ever tour game in 1907, when the visiting New Zealand touring team opened their historic tour with a game against Bramley.

Bramley had a proud history. Formed in 1879 they had some of the best rugby union players in England in the 1890s including England international Harry Bradshaw. Bradshaw worked locally in the textile industry and unlike some of his middle-class team-mates in the England team, could not afford to lose wages by not working Saturday morning, let alone the three days off that an England rugby trip to Dublin would entail. There was no Ryan Air in those days.

So Bramley were instrumental in launching the first challenge to the Rugby Football Union at Twickenham in 1893, over the question of 'broken-time' payments. The challenge failed but two years later some northern rugby clubs broke away to form the Northern Union giving us the sport of rugby league we love today. Bramley did not join the NU in 1895 but did the following year to enjoy 104 years in the professional game before the club was suddenly closed in 1999, the then owners quitting the rugby league.

Bramley had never been one of the top clubs, but became a key player in some quite historic rugby league occasions and events.

Most rugby league fans would be unaware that the club was the first to challenge the Rugby Football Union, as outlined above. The subject of that challenge, Harry Bradshaw, enjoyed the same celebrity status accorded to David Beckham today. When Bradshaw married a Bramley girl in the local church, thousands turned out to see it, with many of the females of the area creating the sort of scenes normally associated with pop stars today.

Bramley were involved in the first ever transfer fee of £100, when they sold Jim Lomas to Salford in the 1901-2 season, a massive figure in those days. And that first ever tour game in 1907 put Bramley in pride of place not only on the English rugby league map, but ensured them a special place in the hearts of New Zealand Rugby League, who keep a copy of the original match programme under glass at the game's headquarters in Auckland. Indeed, the NZRFL have a nominal share in the new Bramley club and will be present at the unveiling of a heritage blue plaque on the wall of the Barley Mow pub, commemorating the historic event.

I have a special interest in French rugby league, but I was unaware until fairly recently that Bramley made a key contribution to the development of the game across the Channel. Bramley chairman, Walter Popplewell, was chairman of the Northern Rugby League at the time of the discussions to establish the game there in the 1930s. But on an even more practical note, when Jean Galia brought his first ever French rugby league pioneers to England, it was Bramley who contributed players to the French side as they were decimated by injuries. They were given French assumed names of course, but they were Bramley lads.

Bramley were often in the shade of both Leeds and Hunslet in the city, who for decades were both regarded as 'big clubs', and in the 1920s and 1930s Bramley chairmen asked: "Do the people of Bramley really want professional rugby league?" But Bramley did enjoy their 'day in the sun' in 1973, and the event was to prove dramatically historic.

The BBC2 Floodlit Trophy had been introduced as a midweek televised competition. After finally obtaining floodlights Bramley were keen for a share of the rewards. Following victories over Wakefield, Castleford and then the mighty St Helens in the semi-final, Bramley were due to meet Widnes in the Final. But it was the year of the miners' strike and power cuts, and floodlit sport was prohibited by Government edict. Instead agreement had been reached for the games to be played in the afternoon and shown at night. A week after disposing of Saints 13-7 in the semi-final, Bramley lost heavily, 27-6 at Widnes in the League. So with Widnes having won the toss for home advantage in the final, Bramley were the underdogs as they travelled to Naughton Park on 18 December. But all Bramley fans can quote the score and name the team that took the club's only major trophy by 15-7. It was no fluke.

23

Bramley were in the First Division, had led the table briefly, also reaching the John Player semi-final and secured their First Division place with a win over Leeds at Headingley in April 1974. Without doubt they were easily the second club in the city of Leeds, the once mighty Hunslet almost facing oblivion as the Parkside ground was sold for warehousing, and a new club - New Hunslet - hastily put together to salvage the traditions of the south Leeds side.

Yes, it was good to be a Bramley supporter. It couldn't last of course, just as Bramley itself was changing, the old main street of Yorkshire stone buildings being replaced by concrete centres and new housing, making newcomers wonder where the team's Villagers nickname came from, and Bramley started to resemble any other suburb of Leeds.

Just like Hunslet the spectre of extinction was to threaten the grand old club. The McLaren Field ground, where the club had moved to, was finally sold by the then directors, after long public debate over planning permission. The club played on at the tidy ground for some years as the wrangling continued, before planning permission was finally approved for houses to be built. Now old Bramley fans still feel a shudder as they pass the crassly named McLaren Fields housing estate, a site which once echoed to the cheers of thousands. The Barley Mow pub is still there, literally next door. The move from the Barley Mow to McLaren Field had been a move of less than 100 yards. Remnants of the legendary dressing rooms are still in the pub, for in the old days the players changed there.

Once the ground had been sold the facilities deteriorated until the club was forced to move, firstly playing at Clarence Field, Kirkstall, the ground of the former Headingley RUFC, before moving to Headingley. The club had a strong side at Headingley, by dint of the Leeds Rhinos link, but its stay there was short-lived and it was announced in late 1999 that the club was withdrawing from the rugby league competition.

Fans were stunned. There had been no inkling of this. The club did not appear to be in any financial difficulties, and indeed was looking forward to the highest income in the club's history with £300,000 due over three years from the recent Sky Television settlement.

At the time Gateshead and Hull were being merged as were Huddersfield and Sheffield, and fans were asking if there were any connections between these events.

A supporters' meeting was called in the Old Vic pub in Bramley and fans expressed their determination not to give up without a fight. Efforts were made to persuade the former directors to reconsider but when this failed, fans were persuaded by the then *TGG!* magazine editor Lee Spracklen to form their own supporters-run club and try to re-enter to the rugby league.

Yes we are related. Lee is my eldest son, and along with brother Karl was a 'Bramley lad', both having been brought up in the area. Being a 'modern' sort of father, I firmly believed that I should play a significant role in their upbringing. So in a noble gesture to give my wife, Maggie, some respite from constantly looking after boisterous lads, I volunteered to take them out on a Sunday, giving her some peace for a few hours. And like any good father I took them to rugby league, which by the time my sons arrived had increasingly moved to Sunday for its games.

Being underpaid, like so many of my hardworking generation, I looked for the cheapest option. So Bramley it had to be. I could push them both in a pushchair up the hill, the mile or so to McLaren Field. If the weather was fine and I was feeling flush I could take them further afield, though being a non-driver it meant by bus or train. This included Hunslet but also other bigger clubs if Bramley or Hunslet were not playing.

At the toddler stage I could not claim that they were rugby league anoraks, so grounds where they could run around were preferred, so a packed Headingley was lower down the preferred list. When they were old enough to appreciate the game they too became hooked, with Karl having a slight preference for Hunslet and Lee for Bramley. In 1978 the atmosphere in the house was incredible. Hunslet and Bramley were neck and neck for promotion to Division 1, and they still had to play each other home and away.

Though only six and eight years old respectively, both knew that this was crunch time. I remember the Leeds Met special buses being run to the games, something more often associated with the then very successful Leeds United. To the satisfaction of all, Hunslet won the game at the Leeds Greyhound Stadium, while Bramley won at McLaren Field. And more importantly, both were promoted. Karl continued his affinities when he reported on games at Hunslet and Bramley for both rugby league weekly papers, in between stints at Cambridge University, at which time he turned out for the newly created Cambridge Eagles team in pre-Rugby League Conference days. Lee, as well as being a fan was a volunteer for the Bramley club when they played at Headingley. Having played for Stanningley, Hunslet Boys Club and captaining local college side Airedale and Wharfedale, who played in the Student Rugby League competition, Lee was passionate about the place of rugby league in the local community.

He was devastated when Bramley suddenly withdrew from the league in 1999 with no explanation, even more so as things were going well on the field, and apparently financially, despite the controversial move to play at Headingley. This was the period when it looked like Gateshead Thunder and Sheffield Eagles might be on their way out as a result of the previously mentioned mergers. As editor of the Rugby League Supporters Association magazine *The Greatest Game!* he was also a champion of ordinary supporters and was not going to take this without comment.

The RLSA and *TGG!* launched a campaign in support of fans of Gateshead, Sheffield and Bramley who were fighting for their clubs in a much publicised Fans Forum at Salford in front of panellists Neil Tunnicliffe and Nigel Wood, who sat alongside three evocative empty chairs, draped respectively with shirts from Gateshead, Sheffield Eagles and Bramley. Then at a historic meeting of Bramley fans at the Old Vic pub in Bramley, Lee was elected chair of first the Bramley Rugby League Action Group, then the Bramley Rugby League Community Club. The model proposed was of a co-operative organisation, owned by fans and the people of Bramley.

Lee was determined that the club could not be bought or sold like the previous Bramley club, the ownership of which had changed hands several times in the past. Old Bramley fans like Martyn Cheney, now club secretary, Nigel Brayshaw, Dave Cromack, Steve Crossley and Tony Greaux became part of the new set-up. All were well known on the clubs' supporters' network following the old club, and all of them were local. Now all were to be directors of the new club.

The new club tried twice to enter the Rugby Football League's Northern Ford Premiership. The first time it was rejected because the chosen stadium, Farsley Celtic AFC did not then meet RFL criteria. Subsequently the club's proposal to play matches at Morley RFC was also rejected, not because of ground criteria, but because of opposition from other clubs, notably Hunslet, who expressed the view that Bramley would be "stepping on their catchment area". Bramley fans who had happily hosted Hunslet for a season at McLaren Field before the latter's move to the brand new South Leeds Stadium still feel that this attitude showed a lack of sportsmanship.

As someone who had worked with Hunslet in the past and as a trustee of the Hunslet Boys Club, which had seen players such as Mick Shoebottom, Jason Robinson, Sonny Nickle, Darryl Cardiss and Chev Walker pass through its doors, I felt especially disappointed.

But Bramley did make it back when a decision was made to apply for entry to National League Three, where the criteria are less demanding. The new Bramley club was accepted into NL3 for the 2004 season, and the club's return was welcomed by more than 1,200 fans as they kicked off at the splendidly appointed ground of Stanningley SARLC against Sheffield Hillsborough Hawks.

The club's catchphrase "Amber and black, fighting back" was justified, in that Bramley were back and with a vengeance.

The inaugural season saw the Bramley Buffaloes average a crowd of 633 a game, quite remarkable for a league in which visiting fans are rare because of the long distances travelled.

The club had adopted the Buffaloes name after heated debates. Wedged geographically between the Bulls and the Rhinos it was agreed that the club needed a strong image to match. Bramley fans, like the buffalo, had become an endangered species, and the club plays 'out west' in Leeds. So it fitted, and was accepted by fans to such an extent that the club mascot Billy Buffalo is much sought after at public and social events in west Leeds, often lining up on the VIP

27

platform alongside Ronnie Rhino. And he out-drank Ronnie Rhino and Bradford's Bullman in one notorious competition.

The creator of the Buffalo logo throws an interesting slant on what is meant by support of a sports club. Rob Wilkinson, now marketing director for Bramley is from West Bromwich, a Yam-Yam as neighbours from Birmingham would say, a fan of the Baggies, West Bromwich Albion FC. Having played rugby union at county level he then tried rugby league at university. Being a convert to the game he needed a club to support, and that was to be Bramley Buffaloes, Rob being attracted by the supporters-run ethos that prevailed at the new club, an ethos that has attracted new fans from as far afield as the home counties.

Attempts were made to ensure that Rhinos' and Bulls' fans were made to feel welcome at Bramley games, but Bramley fans do feel that they are a breed apart. The fans literally own the club, there being several hundred shareholders each entitled to one vote, irrespective of their financial contribution. The club has a much higher marketing profile than previous Bramley clubs, producing a weekly newsletter and having pages in the local press.

Bramley is not currently competing with neighbouring Super League clubs but is already gaining a reputation as a club that players want to join. The club sells itself to new players by offering them a chance to put themselves in the shop window for bigger clubs. That four of the first season's squad were offered lucrative contracts elsewhere is testimony to the success of that approach. We were just 40 minutes away from a Grand Final place as we led Coventry Bears in the semi-final, until an injury to chief playmaker Mark Gibson cost us a fairy tale ending to our first season back.

But fans are delighted just to see a Bramley team run out in the famous amber and black shirts, and whatever the reasons for supporting Bramley in the past, be it geography, the 'underdog syndrome' or the beer in the Barley Mow, Bramley fans with their determination not to see the Bramley name disappear from the rugby league map can justifiably say Bramley is our club. After all, they own it.

5. Carlisle

Alan Tucker recalls a memory concerning his favourite team, which will never be erased even though he probably wishes the score could be.

As a St Helens lad, I have so many great memories such as Tom van Vollenhoven's first try as a St Helens player, and that fantastic try at Wembley in 1961, when his interpassing with Ken Large from his own 10-yard line led Saints to victory in the Challenge Cup Final over Wigan.

The memory that's etched deepest in my consciousness also involves Saints after I had just joined the board of Carlisle RLFC, having moved north in 1971.

It was a glorious September afternoon in 1986. Carlisle's new coach Roy Lester had just had a major clear out of most of our travelling Yorkshire-based players, we had recruited a couple of New Zealanders and we were confident of at least giving the Saints a competitive game.

We were absolutely hammered. Twenty tries with 16 goals left the score at 112–0. Twelve Saints players scored tries with, from memory, Neil Holding and Barry Ledger getting four each.

Some bizarre recollections of that horrible day include: Alex Murphy screaming at his players to "run at the midgets in the middle"; one of the Saints directors moaning throughout the second half about a try that had been disallowed, and a bus-load of Carlisle supporters who sang "We'll support you evermore" right through to the final whistle.

The Monday evening edition of the local Carlisle paper beneath the headline "Slaughter under the sun" carried the opening lines that I'll never forget. "Carlisle did some things right on Sunday. No-one missed the bus and their shirts looked clean and well pressed."

Strangely enough, the team recovered and went on to finish in the top half of the old Division 2 table.

Bramley versus Leeds at Barley Mow, around 1950.
(Photo: Robert Gate)

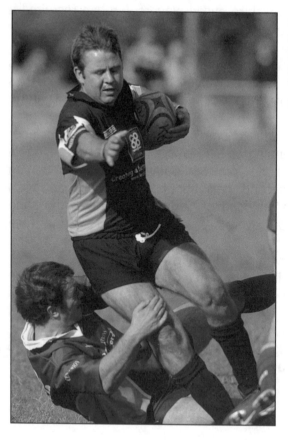

Marc Gibson in
action for Bramley
Buffaloes
(Photo: David
Williams,
rlphotos.com)

6. Halifax RLFC

I remember watching the 1987 Challenge Cup Final when Halifax defeated St Helens by one point at Wembley.

Also, 12 months later I found myself at Wembley cheering on Wigan against Halifax. As quite a newcomer to the sport I was a little bit overawed at the whole occasion, but the Halifax fans were absolutely fantastic and they made it such a special day. I will never forget my first time at Wembley.

Unfortunately in recent years Fax have had both financial worries and been relegated from Super League. As a result some fans have stopped going to the Shay, but the majority still follow their club.

Over the years Halifax have signed a number of world-class players and have won quite a number of trophies. Some great stars have graced both Thrum Hall and The Shay including Tyssul Griffiths, Johnny Freeman, Bruce Burton, Keith Williams, Ronnie James, Brendan Hill, John Schuster, Graham Eadie, John Pendlebury, Chris Anderson, Greg Florimo, Gavin Clinch and Martin Pearson.

Halifax fan John Starr has followed the blue and whites since 1982 and also loves to write poetry.

A Halifax fan from London

I was brought up in London's East Ham in the 1960s. One of my earliest memories is sitting with my grandmother in front of our television set on a Saturday afternoon.

She and I were huge wrestling fans. Kent "have a good week, till next week" Walton was our host on ITV's *World of Sport*. We were enthralled by the antics of the likes of Steve Logan, Mick McManus and Jacky Pallo.

With only two black and white television channels to choose from, the BBC had to try to entice viewers to watch their programmes in preference to ITV.

So, on a winter's Saturday afternoon, straight after the motorcycle scrambling, I first encountered rugby league, in all its black and white glory.

Often in the rain and mud both teams were indistinguishable from each other. But I wasn't bothered because I had a commentator to guide me through this foreign game, and what a commentator he was, what a voice.

The man in question, Eddie Waring, made me love the greatest game of all. Because I lived in the East End of London, his rich Yorkshire accent was the first I had ever heard. I can still hear him now; I listened to him for years.

He was the voice of the Challenge Cup, and when he eventually fronted BBC2's Floodlit rugby league I was hooked. Towards the end of his career many observers thought his accent was demeaning to the game, and maybe it was, but he was well loved by many more, including me.

That could have been the end of it, but in 1982 life offered me the toss of a coin and I had a choice between accepting a job in Billinge in Lancashire, or one in Halifax in West Yorkshire. Had I gone to Billinge I could have enjoyed decade of unbeatable Wigan at Wembley, or maybe a life of following St Helens, but no... I chose the job in Halifax.

Even then I didn't go to a game for six years. Then a family friend who was a Halifax supporter offered to take me to a game at Thrum Hall. I stood in the scratching shed and was hooked once again. Yet like so many, my friend no longer goes to the games.

Home and away I took my two daughters to the matches. It was still a winter game then, and with Thrum Hall having one of the highest altitudes for a rugby league ground it was often bitterly cold, with the biting wind seemingly coming straight over the North Sea from the Arctic.

I recall one January evening game when the visiting Widnes side included a warrior from the South Seas who went by the name of Emosi Koloto. He was a huge man, but had never encountered snow and ice before. By the end of the game he was almost immobile with the cold.

All things must come to an end, and so it proved for our 111 years at Thrum Hall. The final match was not to be missed and all the players wore a special long sleeved 'old time' shirt with the old HRLFC crest on its left breast and the newer modern crest on the right.

On the back were the old style consecutive numbers in bold bright red against a solid white square. They were up for grabs after the game for a mere £150 each. I had to have one, I chose the full-back's number one shirt. It was not until

I read the match programme that I realised I was in fact sponsoring a player for the day and was to be presented with the shirt by the wearer himself.

Damien Gibson wore the shirt that day, I was just hoping that he wouldn't damage my shirt. He even had the cheek to bleed on it when he copped a hard tackle. Back in the Taverners' Club I received the now signed shirt from Gibbo himself. It is the most expensive single piece of clothing I own, it was worth every penny and I still wear it with pride.

I had often been into the Taverners Club and had seen the decades of sepia-toned photographs of old players. I readily recognised the more recent players' photographs. The muse came upon on me and I wrote a short poem based on these photographs.

I bought a square of Thrum Hall grass during the very last days of our beautiful, sloping, idiosyncratic pitch. Many months after the ground was sold I returned to look over the old pitch for one last time. I shouldn't have gone back, the local vandals had been at work and I could have cried after seeing what had become of the old place.

Thrum Hall is Dead, Long Live the Shay.

These walls are our history, these photographs proud,
Crested jackets, creased trousers, sepia hoops never loud,
A better time, it is said, was this past foreign land,
But our slope was deceiving, gales froze the hands,
Part-time gentleman players, they all did their share,
Looking smart in their suits, with slicked-back bryl-creamed hair,
There've been hundreds of men, never once did they slack,
Yet some lights shone brighter, fond thoughts looking back,
Kielty's 12 glorious winters stand him up there alone,
An ebony tornado set Freeman's try tally in stone,
Sure-footed Ron James, ever-present with flair,
A thousand goals never bettered, ancient boots he did wear,
We were hoarse on emotion when Andersons' boys made us weep,
All heroes of Wembley, built on team spirit so deep,
The flying Mark Preston, check the fax, he did soar,
Yet this prolific try scorer was never destined to roar,
Big Brendan piledriving towards green and gold lines,
Mesmerising Greg Austin, to be savoured like wine,
Pacific warriors came too, travelling far from their isles,
Fearsome bronzed tribesmen, belying their smiles,

The side-stepping John Schuster kicked straight as a rod,
Racked up goal upon goal, his boots kissed by a God,
Quicksilvered collisions, hard knocks like before,
Full of grace, skill and beauty, men joined in a war,
It's quick and it's sly, always breathless in pace,
Hard yards by the inch, looking fear in the face,
Now the batons been passed from Thrum Hall to the Shay,
Don't forget our past glories, they'll keep bad times at bay,
Here's to the wags in the shed, to the pride of the town,
They'll follow forever, so don't let them down,
They'll chant, clap and sing, like they did in the past,
You've given your all, so will we, to the last.

June Sharp from Crowle, North Lincolnshire has been following rugby league for more than 60 years and outlines her fondest memories.

Third generation Halifax fan

I remember my mother holding me in front of a picture, pointing to rugby players and getting me to say their names – it was a picture of the 1939 Halifax team which won the Challenge Cup beating Salford in the Final.

My mother was taken to watch Halifax by her father in 1910-11 when a male Halifax member could take a female to watch the game for free. They lived about a mile away from Thrum Hall and he would stand at the gate watching the crowd pass through the end of the street, while waiting for the ladies to get ready. My grandpa would walk to Huddersfield to support Halifax.

My earliest memories were of waiting for my brother to come home from Wembley. He went on the train and was very excited when he returned home with several sports papers.

From the age of 11, I watched Halifax and sometimes went to the away games with my brother. We went by bus, changing at Cleckheaton bus station. This was an uncertain way of travelling because the buses often came in full and "three only" would be announced, but we always seemed to squeeze on.

My brother bought a second-hand car, and as Halifax entered into the Lancashire League we started to travel to

Lancashire for away games. I remember following our team to Hull once and not daring to cheer when our team scored, we actually hid our hand-knitted blue and white scarves under our coats.

There was a high wire fence at Hull in front of the stand in case the crowd became annoyed and began hurling missiles. Our team won there once and we dashed to see them come off the field. Jack Wilkinson, who had played a blinder was chased off and things were being thrown at him, however we didn't mind because we had won. I now knew why all the changing room windows had wire grills across them.

We didn't just go to see Halifax, another good game was at Hunslet. I saw Lewis Jones there in his early career. With me being small I couldn't see in a large crowd so my brother hoisted me up on top of the turnstile gate in front of the paddock.

Later on, my brother became a director of Halifax and in 1964 together with a fellow 'fax director helped to reform Bradford Northern.

When I got married, my mother and brother left the wedding reception to and watch Halifax versus St Helens. That was, of course, acceptable as we plan all our family activities and holidays around rugby league. My mother used to buy my three sons schoolboy passes for Bradford, a team we now follow and our whole family go to the games. I've seen some wonderful matches, fantastic tries and magnificent defence play. I love all aspects of the game, including the banter between spectators, but turn a deaf ear to the bad language.

I've followed my team to Australia for the World Club Championships, been to internationals, student games, seen the Aboriginal tour games, and visited almost every rugby league ground.

Yet my proudest moment in rugby league was when my 12-day-old grandson came to the Challenge Cup semi-final in 2003, then onto Cardiff for the final. Rugby league is thrilling and I shall follow the sport live for as long as I can.

Halifax versus Hull at Thrum Hall on 23 March 1963.
(Photo: Courtesy Robert Gate)

Halifax versus Workington at Thrum Hall on 20 August 1960.
(Photo: Courtesy Robert Gate)

Left: Halifax hero Jack Wilkinson at Wembley for the 1956 Challenge Cup Final.
(Photo: Courtesy Robert Gate)

Right: Leigh versus Featherstone at Hilton Park 19 March 1955
(Photo: Courtesy Robert Gate)

Hull versus Bradford at The Boulevard 7 November 1976
(Photo: Courtesy Robert Gate)

Hull versus Halifax at The Boulevard in 2000, with the Threepenny
Stand in the background. (Photo: Peter Lush)

7. Hull FC

Hull FC has some of the most loyal and passionate fans in world sport, never mind rugby league.

The followers of the Airlie Birds have turned out in their thousands for years, and all away fans would have commented about the atmosphere that was generated from the threepenny stand at their old Boulevard home.

The club was founded in 1865 and won countless trophies and honours over the years.

Over the years the black and whites have seen some of the greatest players tread the hallowed turf of the Boulevard and now the KC Stadium, including such stars as Billy Batten, Jack Harrison, Joe Oliver, Clive Sullivan, David Topliss, Steve 'Knocker' Norton, Peter Sterling, Gary Kemble, James Leuluai, Garry Schofield, Lee Crooks, Lee Jackson, Jason Smith and Richard Horne.

Dean Hoggard has infuriated his girlfriend over the years of his love affair, or maybe obsession, with rugby league.

Hull at Old Trafford

I've supported Hull FC since about 1982. My grandad started taking my older brother into the famous Threepenny Stand at the Boulevard and soon after I followed.

I could talk all day about my memories of Hull FC but some of my favourites include our championship winning side doing the Haka in front of the Threepenny Stand.

An amusing memory is when an old guy's false teeth fell on my brother's shoulder after a Hull try, I will never forget that.

I also remember when inflatable objects were the current craze in sport and I decided to take my inflatable skeleton wrapped in a Hull shirt and scarf. I was well chuffed when I saw myself with the skeleton on ITV's *Scrum Down*. I was also on *Scrum Down* dancing around behind Roger Millward after the local derby match with Hull KR.

My best memory though has got to be standing with the Hull fans packed into Old Trafford in 1991, singing our heads off and unable to move because of the big attendance. We were watching unfancied Hull FC beat the all-star Widnes team to lift the Premiership trophy.

Every time Widnes' Martin Offiah got the ball we thought he was going to go the full length of the pitch, but he didn't. What a day.

Jayne Ball has followed rugby league since 1982, and explains how married life made her swap Hull for Leeds.

From Hull to Leeds

In 1982, I was 20 years old and had never watched a rugby league match, despite living in a city that was famous for Hull FC and Hull KR. This information was my only knowledge of rugby league. My sister and brother-in-law, on the other hand, were - and still are - rugby league mad.

At this time my sister Karen was pregnant with her second child but when Hull FC reached the Challenge Cup Final, there was no way she was not going to Wembley. It was decided that I should accompany the supporters to keep Karen company in the long, long queue for the ladies' toilets. This was the 1980s when the crowd regularly topped 90,000.

In keeping with tradition, on the morning of the Final I was kitted out in a black and white scarf, rosettes, badges, plastic top hat and several stickers, I particularly remember one referred to Trevor Skerrett. I was oblivious to the fun and dreaded to think what I looked like. The coach dropped us off at the stadium and I clearly remember weaving our way through all the parked coaches, one hand securing the plastic top hat and trying to keep up with my excited relatives. Suddenly there was a shout "they're here... look, they're here." Confused I stopped and still pressing the plastic hat firmly to my head, looked up into the passing coach. It was the team bus, I copied everyone else and waved frantically at the men inside and one very handsome chap even waved back.

After the predicted long visit to the ladies, we took our place in the stand and on examining the programme I was chuffed to discover that the mystery 'waver' was in fact Gary Kemble, our full-back.

The match is a bit of a blur, a mixture of watching the game while trying to listen to the rules from Karen and Rob - the running commentary must have driven the folks around us mad. But what I do remember is the excitement, the tension, cheers and apprehension. How could anyone go to a rugby league final at Wembley, especially one which ends in a draw and not be hooked for life?

After that I went to loads of matches at the Boulevard. My favourite player was the amazing Australian scrum-half Peter Sterling, I thought anything was possible when he was playing. Then in 1987 I married and moved to Sherburn near Leeds, and we always seemed too busy to fit in a visit to watch Hull. However, Hull's star player Garry Schofield also moved over to Leeds, followed by Lee Crooks and Gary Divorty. We were interested to see what was happening at Headingley and we decided to pay them a visit. Before we knew it we had committed the gravest of sins – we became Rhinos supporters, or Loiners, as they were known then.

In 1988 it was my turn to be pregnant and we went to Elland Road to see Leeds play in the Yorkshire Cup Final. Garry Schofield took the ball near his own line and desperately ran the full length of the pitch. My husband, Philip, and I yelled, "Go on, go on, go on," willing Garry to run faster and score... and he did. A few months later these words greatly irritated me as Philip shouted them once more, in the same tone, when I was in labour. The midwife was calmly giving me the instructions during the delivery but all I could think was: "Philip thinks I'm Garry Schofield running the length of Elland Road again".

So here we are now, Rhinos fans, and although I love my sister and her family dearly, we seldom agree where rugby league is concerned.

Keighley Cougars – Divisional Premiership winners at
Old Trafford in 1995. (Photo: Courtesy Robert Gate)

Leigh fans at the Northern Ford Premiership Final against
Dewsbury in 2000. (Photo: Peter Lush)

8. Keighley Cougars

Darren Mabbot is a Keighley fan, but he also follows another team by the name of Cougars.

I am a big rugby league fan and I support two teams in the greatest game, the first one is Keighley Cougars, they are my home town team.

My dad took me to my first game in 1990, to see a match against Rochdale Hornets. I have supported Keighley ever since, through good times and bad. I remember some of the great players who have worn the red, white and green of Keighley - players like Ian Gateley, Simon Irving, Andy Eyres, Nick Pinkney, Steve Hall and many others.

Some of the greatest moments in that time are the Championship winning seasons of 1992-93 and 1994-95, the Premiership win in 1994-95 and beating Salford after being 10 points down at the Willows. These provided me with some really great times.

The second team I support are the Canada Cougars. I grew up in Canada and when I read about rugby league being played in Canada I wanted to be their biggest fan. I remember going to Cougar Park in Keighley and watching them lose 66-6 to Italy, in the Emerging Nations World Cup in 2000. The highlight of the tournament was the game they won against Japan, which stopped them from being awarded the wooden spoon.

I hope to be able to keep following them, and hope the international rugby league board can sort themselves out, so teams like Canada can play regular rugby league.

Jason Barnett is another Cougar and has seen the good and bad times over the past couple of decades. Here he explains how he copes with living in the shadow of Bradford and supporting Keighley.

Third generation Keighley fan

I am now 28 years old and have been watching Keighley Cougars since I was four years old. My dad Roger is also a keen Keighley fan and his grandad before that.

I got into rugby after I watched it with my dad as a youngster and totally fell in love with the game. I enjoyed it so much I ended up playing for Keighley Cougars' junior teams right up to the age of 18 before having to pack it in due to injury.

Rugby league is the greatest game and is a working man's game, unlike other sports.

My earliest rugby league memory was around 1985 when Keighley were struggling for money and players. We were playing Fulham at Lawkholme Lane; it was a wet and windy day with only around 500 fans bothering to turn up. At full time, Fulham's dressing room lights had packed in, and because it was winter they ended up getting changed in an old bar under the main stand. The Fulham team could not have been happy, but that was how poor Keighley were in those days.

My fondest memory has to be when we clinched the Stones Bitter Division 3 title in the 1992-93 season, our first trophy for 100 years.

I remember the night we won it, we had to beat Batley at Cougar Park to clinch the title. It was an evening kick-off and the pitch was waterlogged and thick with mud - to be honest the match should have been called off. Thankfully it wasn't and we overcame Batley to be crowned champions.

Peter Roe, our coach then, had masterminded the season and because he was a Keighley lad and former player, he was over the moon.

After the full-time hooter he was dumped in the mud by the players as a joke, which was great fun. That night there were 5,600 people present, the biggest crowd I have seen at Keighley in my 24 years. But in 2005 we were struggling to get 1,000 spectators at games – where did all those fans go?

When we were denied Super League status in 1995 after winning promotion was a very sad time for Keighley as a whole, because we had won the league easily. The club certainly suffered as a result.

9. Leeds Rhinos

After 32 years of hurt and being labelled as chokers Leeds Rhinos finally lifted the most coveted prize in rugby league.

On Saturday 16 October 2004, the Rhinos claimed the Super League title beating the Bradford Bulls 16-8 at Old Trafford. And four months later the Rhinos overcame the Canterbury Bulldogs to become the World Club Champions.

It has taken a long time for Leeds to be taken seriously as title challengers and with Tony Smith at the helm the Rhinos have become a major force.

Over the years the club have had some great players including Fred Webster, Lewis Jones, Eric Harris, Garry Schofield, Lee Crooks, Ellery Hanley, Andy Gregory, Iestyn Harris and Adrian Morley.

Una Dennett, from Cornwall is a Londoner with a passion for the Rhinos, and once had a slight obsession with Iestyn Harris – not sure if that passion is still there now he is a Bull, but never mind. She once suggested moving home because of rugby league.

Long distance Rhino

I am a 64-year-old grandmother and have not participated in any sport since my schooldays. I watched my kids if they played, but even then I wasn't much of a spectator.

Television coverage of tennis or athletics sometimes caught my interest, but not very often. I am a Londoner and my husband comes from Widnes, but he had never been a fan of rugby league despite living opposite the Widnes ground.

Anyway, in early 1998 my youngest son was working at The Stoop in Twickenham for Harlequins rugby union club and my husband was helping him out here and there. One weekend he asked me if I would like to go to the ground to watch a game. Thinking it would make a change from my usual routine, I agreed. I was amazed to find the game was London Broncos versus Halifax because I'd assumed it was going to be a union game. By half-time I was totally hooked.

I told Roy, my husband, that I wanted to see some more of this league game. He pointed out to me that living in London would make it difficult as it was primarily played up north.

I didn't realise it at the time but the game I'd just watched put the Broncos into a semi-final with Wigan for a place in the Challenge Cup Final. The game was to be played at Huddersfield. "Ok", said Roy: "I'll take you to the McAlpine Stadium." That game really opened my eyes towards rugby league. Wigan looked so fit and strong. Needless to say Wigan won, but obviously I couldn't travel north every weekend to watch games.

I did suggest moving house, but that idea didn't go down to well with the family. So the next thing I did was install Sky Sports, and once that was done there was no stopping me. Anything I could watch I did. More trips up north followed too, to different grounds and teams – it was wonderful. My family thought I'd gone completely mad, in fact they still do.

At this stage I didn't have a favourite team, then I saw Iestyn Harris. That did it for me – I was now a Rhinos fan. You know where Roy had to take me next? Headingley - of course.

Unfortunately about this time I had a recurrence of hip problems I'd suffered with in 1997. My trips round the country had to go on hold. But by now as well as television, I was receiving *Rugby League World* and *League Express* so I was able to follow my passion from home.

We also moved home when we retired. Unfortunately it was not to Leeds though – my first choice - but to Cornwall. So here I am, even further away from the M62 and the game's heartlands. But I've got Sky Sports and my reading material, occasional trips to selected matches in London when I stay with the kids, a trip to Old Trafford in October and Iestyn Harris is back in league – even though he's at Bradford.

My biggest thrill so far was when I took my trip back to Headingley after my second hip operation. We stayed just round the corner from the ground and we took a walk just to see the stadium and Roy got chatting to the man on the gate while I stocked up on Rhinos merchandise in the shop. It turned out that unusually the team was training there that day and he said we could go and watch, which we did. I was so thrilled. Then another chap came over and Roy explained what we were doing there and why, plus how far we had come. He said that it would be alright if I stood where the players would go back in after training, and he said they would probably give us some autographs.

Roy got me a pack of cards from the club shop - probably the ones the kids buy - and I stood excited as a 10-year-old as I accosted the players and asked them to sign my cards. They were all very sweet and obliged. Keith Senior was curious about our presence so I told him that I'd travelled from Cornwall to see them play on the Friday night. He and some of the others laughed and said that I must be "bloody barmy". I said that my husband, family and friends thought so too, but who cares?

Guess what – Iestyn didn't play that game, I think his wife had their baby that weekend. So up until now I still haven't seen him play in a live game.

I really can't imagine my life without my rugby league fix now. There is no sport to beat it. I only wish that it got the kind of audience it deserves. The players and staff all work so hard and don't receive nearly enough credit for it.

It amazes me the coverage other sports get and the praise heaped on their players who seem to be both overpaid and underachieving despite the money and facilities they enjoy.

Steve Brown has only been following the Leeds Rhinos since 1998, but it was love at first sight.

A new fan

I am a relative newcomer to the sport of rugby league and remember exactly how I came to be so in love with the game.

Six years ago a girlfriend of mine asked me when I'd like to meet her dad. My reply was: "Anytime you like my dear" or something similar. I was then invited to Headingley to see Leeds Rhinos versus Castleford. I agreed, and not knowing much about the game, and not wanting to look too much of an idiot, I had a word with a few lads from work, asking for clarification on the game's rules.

Suitably informed, off we went. Her old man was a 'South Stander' and so that's where we stood. I can't describe the feeling when the Rhinos came onto the pitch - electrifying doesn't do it justice. So taken was I with the game that when a Castleford player ran threequarters of the pitch for a try, losing a boot in the process, I screamed and cheered - slap, bang in the middle of the South Stand – resulting in one very unimpressed possible future father-in-law and one livid girlfriend. Was I ashamed, embarrassed even? Well, fortunately that girlfriend shortly became an ex, but my support of Leeds goes from strength to strength.

I have had some fantastic experiences, memories and games since then, but that first game still does it for me. And I just keep my mouth shut whenever I'm in the South Stand.

Douglas Dale lived close to Headingley, so it was obvious he was going to support Leeds – despite not remembering much about his first game.

Sixty years a Loiner

I am 74 years of age, and have been watching rugby league since the middle of the Second World War.

I was born in Leeds, evacuated after the war started in 1939 but returned home in early 1941. I lived at the other side of the city but fortunately on a direct bus route from Harehills to Kirkstall Lane, the cricket side of Headingley. In 1944 someone took me to Elland Road, but I was not too impressed and so tried a match at Headingley. I cannot remember the very first game, but it must have been worthwhile because I was hooked.

The crowds in those days were quite massive, often around 25,000 to 30,000. However, I never felt nervous although I mainly went on my own. I saw many famous players in those early years, Ike Owen was loose-forward for Leeds with Dai Jenkins and Dickie Williams at half-back. Williams was very quick, a ginger-haired wraith. Neighbours Hunslet also had a great rival stand-off, Ginger Burnell, and I recall that I enjoyed the tremendous rivalry as supporters argued over who was the better player.

A favourite ploy at that time, with Leeds anyway, was for the wingers to cross kick for the opposite winger to outflank the opposing full back. Sometimes this worked a treat.

One match in particular lingers thanks to the humour it generated. It was in the 1945-46 season. Leeds were playing Batley and scoring tries but failing to convert them. Batley had a famous full-back called Charlie Eaton who kept Batley in contention with his immaculate kicking. The Batley fans howled their derision every time a Leeds kick failed, but the Leeds lads hit back with "wait till Cookie comes" having just signed the marvellous Bert Cook from New Zealand. He came and was, as the fans predicted, tremendous.

I left home to join the Merchant Navy in 1947 and watching rugby league became sporadic, but I kept in touch via the old *Green Sports Specials* produced by the *Yorkshire Post* on Saturday nights which were always saved for me during that period. I did get to see the wonderful skills of Lewis Jones though, for me the greatest player ever seen, and that includes the great Reg Gasnier from Australia.

Not until I finally settled down in Wakefield in 1980 was I able to see regular games of rugby, and as retirement approached I became a season ticket holder at Leeds around the time Super League began. The game has speeded up tremendously but still does have some terrific skills, particularly in support play. I find it wonderful to be able to attend academy matches and follow the progress of tremendous developing talent at Headingley such as Kevin Sinfield, Rob Burrow and Danny McGuire among so many others. I feel very fortunate in particular because I have been able to bring up my two sons and four grandchildren to enjoy this great game.

Especially enjoyable, of course, was the night-to-be remembered at Old Trafford in October 2004, when at last the Super League Championship was won and brought home to Leeds.

Robert Ismay didn't really think he was ever going to see a rugby league match until he misunderstood his father's plans.

Converted at Parkside

I was de-mobbed from the military in 1947 and had arrived home on a Friday night in May.

After the usual greetings, my father asked if I would like to go to the game on Saturday? "Yes of course I would," was my reply, thinking the 'game' he meant was Leeds United playing at Elland Road.

When Saturday arrived my father said: "As it's a nice day let's walk". After 20 minutes I said: "This isn't the way to Elland Road." He replied we were not going to Elland Road, we were going to Parkside to see Hunslet play Leeds.

Well, it was with some reluctance that I went into the ground. But to put things in a nutshell, I went into the ground a 'heathen' and came out 'converted'. Converted to the greatest, most passionate and exciting game that ever was or ever will be.

Matthew Wharton enjoys supporting Leeds

I am 14 years old and have supported the Leeds Rhinos since the age of seven.

I love rugby league because it is an up-and-coming sport and I enjoy the coverage the BBC do of the Challenge Cup and the Super League Show.

In my opinion it is a brilliant sport and is much better than football, because players can run 100 yards to score a try. It can also be rough, but most of all there is hardly any fighting in the crowd and I can stand with opposing fans and have a bit of banter singing with them.

10. Leigh Centurions

John Lally has been a Leigh fan for 53 years. He tells us about his heroes in red and white and how he enjoyed playtime fights with his hated enemies – Wigan supporters.

My first match was back in 1953 when my dear old dad took me to Kirkhall Lane to watch Leigh versus Barrow when I was nine. I remember that Leigh won easily and there was a very large crowd that day. After that I saw a lot of matches with my dad and then, from the age of 11, I became a Leigh fanatic going every week home and away. Life was simpler in those days: Saturday games, home one week, away the next, if we couldn't afford the away game we would watch the 'A' team at Leigh.

The 'A' team in those days would also attract massive crowds, but I must say my mum and dad would make sure that I got to all the away matches - mum would go into Leigh on Monday morning to find out how much it was to travel away with the supporters' trips run by John Monk's coaches. There were no motorways then, so a trip to Workington would mean a 7.30am pick up in Lowton, three stops on the way there, two on the way back, and arriving back in Lowton around midnight. My mates and I travelled the length and breadth of Lancashire, Yorkshire and Cumberland to watch our heroes.

I went to school in Golborne and most of the kids were rugby mad like me but the majority of them supported Wigan. I remember the playground battles with the junior pie-eaters were long and bloody as I fought to defend my heroes.

In my 53 years of watching rugby league I have many happy memories, and also some sad ones. I have seen Leigh come very close in the big games, but often remain so far away, so I thought I would choose my stand-out match from my time as a fan.

It was 30 March 1957 at Central Park, and the match was Leigh versus Barrow in the Challenge Cup semi-final. I caught the train with my mates from Golborne station to Wigan Wallgate and joined the throng making their way to Central Park, taking our places behind the posts in the old boy's pen.

We were in no doubt whatsoever that we would soon be booking our trip to Wembley. I can still feel the atmosphere today, almost 48 years later. It was absolutely electric. Barrow set off like a train with their great wingers Lewthwaite and Castle going very close early on, but defence was the order of the day and Leigh held on magnificently. Then we experienced joy of joys with a Brian Fallon drop-goal, which was a very rare occurrence in the 1950s, to put Leigh 2-0 up.

As the seconds ticked away disaster struck, a penalty was awarded to Barrow. We screamed: "Are you blind ref that was never a penalty". Up stepped Joe Ball; we couldn't bear to look, closed our eyes and prayed but it was not to be, and the final score was 2-2. As we made our way back to Wigan bus station we had tears in our eyes. It had been so near yet so far. I couldn't make the replay at Swinton because I was at my grandad's funeral, but I remember my dad trying to get the score off the Home Service on the radio in my auntie's house in Bolton. No one had a telephone or television then so it was the following morning when we knew we had lost, but since then we have of course tasted glory at Wembley. Now I am 61 and have three grandsons and a granddaughter. My grandsons accompany me to matches home and away and if they have the same happy memories of the greatest game of all, my job as a grandad is complete.

11. London

Over the past few years rugby league has grown in London, we now have Harlequins RL (formerly the London Broncos, London Crusaders and Fulham), London Skolars and many amateur clubs such as South London Storm doing our nation's capital proud, hopefully one day we will have all three contesting for honours in the top flight.

Jerry Hall started following Fulham in the early days when they were based at Craven Cottage, and even though he has moved away from London he still has some fond memories.

Fulham RLFC and much more

I had the misfortune to be born in an area of the country which, in 1944, was completely barren as far as rugby league was concerned. This was Coventry, and there were no Bears in those days.

Like my father, I followed association football as a lad, my only glimpses of league being the occasional televised matches with dear old Eddie Waring at the microphone – but whenever I saw it I liked it.

I was 25 years old before I saw my first live game. I read in a newspaper that there were still some tickets available for the 1969 Challenge Cup Final at Wembley between Castleford and Salford, so on a whim I travelled to London to see it.

I was immediately hooked. I did not miss a Challenge Cup Final for the next 30 years, during which I moved to London. It was still my only fix of rugby league every year. I used to stand on the Wembley terraces among the northern supporters thinking: "how lucky these people are, they can watch rugby league every week".

Imagine, then, my ecstatic reaction when Fulham RLFC were formed in 1980. At last I could watch rugby league regularly. I never watched another game of soccer.

I followed Fulham RLFC through their chequered existence as Fulham, London Crusaders and London Broncos – playing at a bewildering succession of football, athletics and rugby union stadiums the length and breadth of London. I hardly ever missed a home game.

The culmination was, of course, reaching the Challenge Cup Final in 1999. Finally I was actually supporting my own team at the famous twin towers.

My memories over 20 years of following London would fill three books, let alone one, but that opening game versus Wigan, the fight to survive during the days of struggle after Fulham FC pulled the plug in 1984, the renaissance culminating in the elevation to Super League in its inaugural season, the dramatic heart-stopping Challenge Cup semi-final victory over Castleford at Headingley, and the Wembley Final - although we were beaten - will live forever in my memory.

Cumbria

In 2002, my wife and I moved to Cumbria, a beautiful area we had visited on countless walking holidays over the years. At last I was living in a traditional hotbed of the game. I now follow Workington Town and I am as avid a supporter as I was when following London. I am ever-present at Derwent Park and desperately hope to see Town regain their glory days.

So why do I watch rugby league: it is not, as yet, totally dominated by money like soccer, where clubs can simply buy success by signing star performers for ludicrous sums of money. It is a hard, honest sport played by superb sportsmen. There is no hiding place on a rugby field. The fans are knowledgeable and appreciate good play by both sides, and do not spend their time fighting one another.

The camaraderie among rival fans is heart-warming and in contrast to soccer, where the so-called supporters have to be segregated because they cannot behave like civilised human beings. This was one of the primary reasons why I was able to turn my back on soccer with no regrets.

The spread of rugby league at all levels into every corner of the land is a success story which is the envy of all other sports, and it is destined to become even more popular. Although our game struggles for its fair share of coverage in the rugby union-dominated national press – they will find it impossible to ignore us as the popularity of our game continues to grow.

Paul Hatt has also seen the highs and lows of the London Broncos, including the days when they were called Fulham. Here he explains his love affair with London.

Why do I follow rugby league?

Quite simply this is an all action sport, physically demanding, and a game played at pace with no lack of skill. The commitment and concentration is total.

It was brought home to me, when attending the Grand Final between Leeds and Bradford. Our seats at Old Trafford were right next to the Rhinos dug-out, so we saw the players coming on and off after their spells of playing time. Once the players sat down to rest, their focus on what was happening in the game was almost frightening to behold. It seemed that they were totally oblivious to anything other than the green playing surface in front of them and the movement of the 26 combatants. It was a privilege to witness it.

How long?

I wish I could claim that I was at Fulham's first historic game against Wigan at Craven Cottage in 1980, but I can't. It wasn't until 12 October that year that I saw my first game of live rugby league, when Huddersfield were the visitors and I was one of a 5,939 crowd.

Despite my lack of real knowledge of the finer points of the game, I was gripped by what I saw. It helped that Fulham ran out winners by 30-7, but I was hooked and so began my rugby league education. Iain MacCorquodale made an impression that day with his performance, as did Ian van Bellen and Reg Bowden. Indeed as I look back now, that squad has attained a special place in my memory, and the names of Tony Karalius, Roy Lester, Mal Aspey, Tony Gurley, Adrian Cambriani and Harry Beverley roll off the tongue.

In 1991 I left London to move north with my wife which opened up another chapter in watching rugby league. Fulham had become the Crusaders and then Broncos as they meandered across the capital. Now based in the north, I saw them as an away fan, something which has not always been the most pleasant of experiences. What it did mean, though, was that I starting going to international matches, War of the Roses fixtures and amateur matches. And it is now 25 years since my first game at The Cottage.

My earliest memory

I owe my earliest memories of rugby league to BBC2 and the second-half action of the Floodlit Trophy. Sitting on the sofa on cold winter evenings in the 1970s, the black and white images from unknown locations burned themselves into my consciousness.

Was it the undulating tones of Eddie Waring or the non-stop action in what seemed very dark and muddy conditions? Who knows? But I know this kid from the south enjoyed the experience. While the games and results are but a blur, one image remains, and that is of games from Knowsley Road and the St Helens RLFC board that was displayed proudly on one of the stands. Funny what sticks in the mind.

My fondest memory

I have two fond memories really, both associated with Fulham and London, and both cup games.

The first is from that historic season of 1980 and the John Player Special fixture against Leeds. Even with my limited knowledge of rugby league, I knew Leeds were a big club with a big reputation. That day a 12,000 crowd filled the ground, and it was the first time a large away contingent had followed their team to the capital. The open terrace seemed to be a mass of amber and blue but, despite their support, the day belonged to the underdogs in an epic game which Fulham won 9-3. The defensive effort that day is the overriding memory, but it was also the feeling that Fulham had arrived and could mix it with the best.

The second comes from the Challenge Cup semi-final in 1999: London Broncos against Castleford Tigers at Headingley. A place in the last Wembley Final before the Stadium's famous towers were demolished was at stake.

I went with a mate who was a Castleford fan and during the first half stood among the Cas faithful as London took the initiative. I had to stifle overwhelming joy as the tries were scored. At half-time, as the Cas fans moved to the other end, I started to believe that London could win. However, back came the Tigers and even the Broncos' Wembley veterans Shaun Edwards and Martin Offiah must have believed one last appearance at the famous old ground was slipping away.

There aren't words to convey the feeling as, with the scores level, Steele Retchless latched onto the ball, found a gap and dived over for the winning try. The emotion was too much, I bounced up and down, then proceeded to run up and down the terraces like a man possessed – we were going to Wembley, my beloved Broncos.

Sadly, in sunny May, the Rhinos forgot to read the script and gave us a painful and heavy beating in the Final. However, the elation of that try at Headingley will stay with me always.

Dave Farrar looks back on becoming a London rugby league supporter.

Reflections on watching rugby league for 40 years

Rugby league is like an old friend. If you are lucky enough to be born in a rugby league community it is your birthright and it is always there for you. If, however, you come to the game as an outsider you will be unlucky if you are not welcomed into the bosom of the game. The game is essentially honest, there are no places for fancy Dans or show-boaters; they will soon be given their comeuppance. It is the same with the supporters, any football-type violence is soon given short shrift, which is why the fans can mingle but can also be passionate and partisan. We know it is only a game but it also part of our lives and part of our community. The gladiatorial-type conflicts earn respect from the onlookers and there is no place for the half-hearted. Anything but full commitment is dangerous and concentration is everything.

There may be some who say 'my team till I die' and I can understand that because I was one for 25 years. But now I know it is 'love the one you're with' as I came to London in 1980 (coincidentally the year Fulham RLFC was born) and my attachments to the original Salford Red Devils fell away bit by bit. I tried to support two sides, but what do you do when they play each other? I tried to support one team each half, the one who needed the points the most, the one who had the ball, the one that was at home - all to no avail. I am now a Londoner, with an interest in Salford's results. Of course, I am now a traitor in the place of my birth, as I was told in no uncertain terms by my uncle 'Red Teddy'. But *c'est la vie*, London is the best soap opera in the game, a real roller-coaster of ups and downs. Supporting the game in London is like being a member of a religious sect in Roman times. Londoners in general only understand football, they have a general understanding of cricket and 'rugby', but you have to explain to all but the most keen sports fan what the differences are, and if you are lucky you may be asked "What ever happened to Fulham?"

Watching the London Skolars is like being a sect within a sect, all the fans know each other and, as they say, misery likes company. The Skolars fans are among the most dedicated in the game and I think they support the club because they support the grassroots ethos of the club.

The creation of Quins RL has created yet another scenario in the capital and it will be fascinating to see how the die-hard League fans mix with their new landlords and become a new League family.

London Skolars club secretary Andrew Jackson outlines how he discovered amateur rugby league and much more.

London Skolars: Getting Involved

As a youngster, I would never have expected to get involved in building a club from grassroots level. Until I moved to London, I'd never been to an amateur rugby league game. Growing up in St Helens within a mile of Knowsley Road, there wasn't really any other side to watch but Saints.

I didn't do much in the way of team sports at school, but got really involved in various sports during my three years at Cambridge University. Although, as one team-mate from that time recently remarked: "Sitting in a boat with a microphone didn't really constitute *playing* sport."

Cambridge wasn't exactly big on rugby league and my time there meant I didn't see a lot of Saints during the Mal

Meninga era. Coming down to London in 1987 and training as an accountant didn't increase my rugby league watching. Fulham were going through a grim patch on the other side of London and it took the appearance of former Saints' captain Harry Pinner in the opposition ranks to finally spur me onto making the trip to Chiswick. I started watching more regularly as they morphed into London Crusaders.

I was still making trips up north to watch St Helens, but as those journeys usually involved suffering another defeat at the hands of the arch enemies at Central Park, I seemed to be taking all the pain of supporting a side with little of the pleasure.

Living in East Ham at the time, I started watching East London, an amateur team who played in West Ham. I enjoyed not having to suffer the nerves of having to actually support a team. They folded after a couple of seasons, but another side set up in Hackney soon afterwards. London Skolars were initially thought of as bit "rah". Who'd ever heard of a Rugby League Student Old Boys side before? I quickly realised that was a misconception and almost considered starting to play until at one game I heard crunching bones as Hemel's Nico Serfontein put in a tackle feet away from me. I quickly realised where my pain threshold lay.

Skolars were playing at Hackney RFC's ground in Clapton at the time which was by the side of the River Lea. Maybe it was seeing boat crews again that made me want to get involved. The club was clearly ambitious and the move to the National Conference League was a big step up.

Central to that ambition was the club founder and chairman Hector McNeil, whose energy and persistence still inspires me nine years later. Hector must have spotted me as a regular at games and initially persuaded me to help out by writing a match report that had go out straight after the game and to write an opinion page for the programme. I'd not got any journalistic experience, but had always enjoyed writing. It was also a nice release from accountancy.

A few months later, the press officer was emigrating and I ended up writing the entire match day programme. Soon afterwards I took over as club secretary. The club had moved to New River Stadium in Wood Green and was playing all year round, having also been one of the movers behind the foundation of the Rugby League Conference. The Conference and the game in the south moving completely to the summer have been fundamental in the growth of the game.

I missed out on the club's trip to Russia and Tatarstan, but a drive up to Wath Brow and back on the shortest day of the year in 1998, was probably when I realised just how committed I'd become to the cause.

Dropping out of the National Conference League was a low point at the time, but the pressures of playing in two competitions whose seasons were starting to overlap was proving impossible. As events have turned out, that move helped us focus and move forwards again.

The move to professionalism and National League 2 was an enormous leap. There were a few times in 2003, our first season, when I wondered why we hadn't just gone for the comfortable option of staying in a lower league and collecting silverware. But the club has never been one for taking easy options and I'm very glad that we've pushed ourselves. As Wayne Bennett says "Don't let the music die in you". We won 41-8 at Dewsbury in 2004 on an afternoon when the biggest cheer came when they announced after an hour that there would be no home man of the match award. That sort of day makes an awful lot of tough ones worthwhile. A pre-season game against Saints was pretty strange for me supporting both clubs, and the 2006 Challenge Cup game against Warrington showed just how far Skolars have come in 11 years, although we lost 52-0.

Visiting clubs with a long tradition and history is always fascinating and hearing stories from former internationals, some of whom I've only ever seen on video is quite humbling at times. The fact that many of them are impressed with the development work we've done in North London shows that we are working in the right direction. It's not a quick job, but I really think we will only beat Australia if we maximise the potential playing base in this country. We've already produced four youth internationals and I'm sure there are many more to unearth.

I've had all sorts of roles at the club, from touch-judging reserve games, timekeeping and press officer. Winning the

Skolars' 'Clubman of the Year' last season was quite a proud moment for me and it can't be often that a club director wins such an award.

When the original guy who did the public address on match days had to drop out suddenly one Sunday afternoon, I stepped into the breach. It's re-energised my love of music, even if my tastes aren't necessarily suitable for match days. The rugby league world is never going to be quite ready for the likes of Ladytron or the Cocteau Twins, but it's always fun to able to play The Fall's *Hit The North* after a win.

So 20 years on from university, I'm still sitting with a microphone whilst other people push themselves to their physical limits and sometimes beyond them. Even as a director, I still have a fan's awe of what the guys are prepared to go through. Being able to get involved in the Skolars and help shape the club, means that I can contribute to getting the players the best chance of success. That's the really satisfying part of my involvement.

Richard Pitchfork is the press officer and a player at South London Storm. He outlines his memories of rugby league.

South London Storm

I originate from Sheffield, and to a family that mostly follows rugby union. The schools I went to all played union as did my local clubs and so union it was for me.

My mother's side of the family, however, originated from Warrington and I grew up hearing brilliant stories from my grandfather of his days at Wilderspool watching Brian Bevan and the rest and going to see the 1954 Challenge Cup Final replay at Odsal.

My first taste of rugby league came in my gap year when a friend asked me to play rugby league for a works team he knew in Wakefield, so off I went to play on the wing for the entire match. I can't remember the score but I do remember having a great time and enjoying every minute of it.

At Birmingham University my first instinct was to play union, but after just two weeks I had got fed up with the people in the club and went to rugby league. I have never looked back, playing first at full-back before moving to the wing and stand-off at university and then becoming a centre just before I left.

From university onwards it has been almost all highs throughout my rugby career and in life in general. Both on and off the pitch rugby league has had a massive effect on me. It has brought me great memories on the pitch, some of the best people I could have wished to meet and even my girlfriend has a rugby league link - she was flatmate with a team-mate's girlfriend.

The highs that stand out for me are numerous but they include: winning the Student Rugby League Nines tournament in Dublin in 1998; the Sheffield Eagles' Challenge Cup Final victory in 1998; captaining the South London Storm 'A' side to their first ever victory in the Rugby League Conference against Hemel Hempstead in 2003; playing for South London Storm in the Challenge Cup in 2003 against West Bowling; playing for South London Storm against the Australian Legends in 2003; playing for the London representative side against Dublin in the Inter-city challenge in 2004 and becoming clubman of the year at South London Storm in 2003.

Probably for me the best of all was playing for South London Storm against Warrington Woolston Rovers at Wilderspool, where my grandfather watched his heroes run out to play.

Alongside these playing highs are those from meeting some of the most active people in the game, with rugby league in their hearts and to count them as friends.

More than anything, league to me is a fraternity, the clubs you join give you the best friends you could want. From university to my present club at South London, I have met some fantastic people both at my own club and others.

I've also seen some of the best acts of human kindness for players such as Bobby Hutton and Matt King who have had the league community rally around them following life-threatening injuries.

How many of these things can many people say they have witnessed or done if not within the rugby league family, for a family it really is. From my grandfather to my friends now, it's a family with similar backgrounds but the same moral outlook and down-to-earth nature. Rugby league truly is the greatest game and not only on the pitch.

I now believe I can help to shape the future of rugby league in London as a press officer as well as a player at South London Storm, as we aim to grow and progress. I'm proud to be involved with the club and the people there.

Peter Lush reflects on what rugby league means to him.

Rugby league changed my life

As a Londoner, prior to the autumn of 1980, rugby league meant very little to me. Football and cricket were my main sporting interests. But then Dave Farrar took me to one of the early Fulham matches at Craven Cottage. At first it was just something to do on a Sunday afternoon – an entertaining spectacle. The skills and passion were apparent, even to a novice supporter like me.

After that memorable first season, we usually went to the home matches and made the occasional trip 'up north'. I became a 'supporter' rather than a 'spectator' as the club went through ups and downs in the 1980s.

Things changed in 1993 when Dave and I had the idea of writing a book about the club, and rugby league in London. The first outline was about 16 pages, *Touch and Go* ended up at a massive 372 pages. We printed 1,100 copies, which sold out in two years.

We then decided to do a guidebook to the rugby league grounds. I spent a week in the north during the wonderful 1995 World Cup, visiting grounds and watching games. Since then, we have published another 23 books about the game, including this one, with more planned. In 2000, we launched *Our Game*, a twice-yearly magazine, looking at the game's history and current issues.

I have had some wonderful experiences through this – meeting and interviewing some of the great players and coaches, learning an enormous amount from talking to others who have researched the sport's fascinating history. One of the highlights was the launch of Harold Genders' book *The Fulham Dream* in 2000, which reunited for the first time since 1984 the original Fulham players.

We did not anticipate in 1993, when we started work on *Touch and Go*, how London League Publications would develop. I am pleased that we have been able to help in the recording of rugby league's history, and to preserve it for future generations. This has included books about Neil Fox, Brian Bevan, Doug Laughton, Trevor Foster and Paul Newlove, but also the work at grassroots level to build the Rugby League Conference and the game in Scotland and Wales. To be able do this has been a privilege.

A special part of our work is still about London. Having the opportunity to talk to some of our players from the past when we published *From Fulham to Wembley* to mark the club's 20th anniversary in 2000 was very special. London's fans have made a unique contribution to the game, and we dedicated that book to Bob Evans, one of London Rugby League's most famous fans, who had died on the morning of the 1999 Challenge Cup Final.

To pick out particular matches from 26 years is very difficult. Some of the wins in the Chiswick period from 1985 to 1989 stand out, if only because we didn't win very often. The first home game in Super League in 1996 against Paris St Germain was also memorable, crowds queuing around The Valley to get in to see our 38-22 win.

The game's heartlands will always be crucial. But what really pleases me comparing rugby league now to 1980 is the enormous development of the game in London, the south, in Wales and internationally. That is the legacy of the launch of Fulham in 1980, and I remain optimistic about the game's potential for growth in the future.

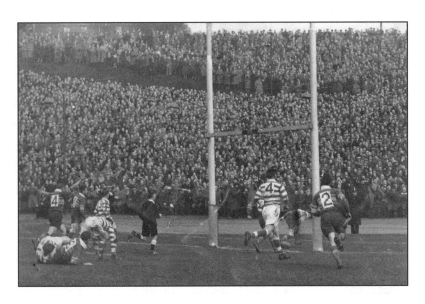

Leeds versus Barrow, Challenge Cup semi-final at Odsal in 1951.
The result was a 14-14 draw in front of 57,729 fans. Barrow won
the replay 28-13, but lost the Final 10-0 to Wigan.
(Photo: Courtesy Robert Gate)

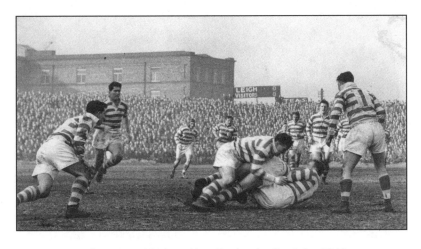

Leeds versus York at Headingley in the late 1940s.
(Photo: Courtesy Robert Gate)

Leigh versus Halifax in the Challenge Cup 28 February 1953. The
result was a 7-7 draw, Leigh won the replay, but lost to
St Helens in the next round.
(Photo: Courtesy Robert Gate)

London Skolars versus York City Knights at New River Stadium
June 2005 (Photo: Peter Lush)

South London Storm versus Australian Legends in 2003.
Jason Hetherington about to receive the ball.
(Photo: Peter Lush)

Lobbying Parliament: Ray Gent presenting The Petition. On his left
is Cliff Spracklen, on his right David Hinchliffe, who at the time was
MP for Wakefield and Secretary of the All-Party Parliamentary
Rugby League Group. (Photo: Peter Lush)

London Broncos celebrate a try at The Valley.
(Photo: Peter Lush)

Harlequins RL versus Castleford March 2006. Lee Hopkins tackles
a Castleford player. (Photo: Peter Lush)

12. St Helens

St Helens are one of the biggest clubs in rugby league. During the 1950s and 1960s Saints were a force to be reckoned with, winning a host of trophies and having a fine squad of players which boasted the likes of Tom van Vollenhoven, Alex Murphy, Alan Prescott and Vince Karalius.

In 1958 six St Helens players managed to make the Great Britain tour of Australia, alongside Prescott, Murphy and Karalius were Frank Carlton, Glyn Moses and Ab Terry.

The Saints faithful are a very passionate band, and their constant singing and chanting make Knowsley Road a fortress to play at.

Since the introduction of Super League, St Helens have been the dominant force in the game winning four Super League titles and they now boast fantastic international players such as double Man of Steel winner Paul Sculthorpe, Paul Wellens, Kieron Cunningham and Sean Long.

Simon Speight, also known as South Wales Saint, now follows the team from afar.

Hooked on Saints

Everyone says you always remember your first live rugby league match, who was playing, what the score was and who won. So I guess I am the exception. Sure, I can remember going to my first game, but nothing of the details.

My first live match must have been some time in the early 1980s. Like most people, I first cut my teeth watching matches on television. My earliest memory is watching a bald Tony Marchant flying down the pitch to score a long-range try for Castleford. I was astounded at the speed of the guy.

However, I first started going to live matches because most of my mates at school were Saints mad, and all they'd talk about on Monday mornings was the Saints match from the previous weekend.

In order to be able to join in with the conversation, I thought I'd better go along. I don't remember much about the game, but they must have won, because my friend's dad told me if they lost, I was walking home. Thankfully, that didn't happen, so Saints saved my poor feet.

Like so many before me, once I'd been to a game, I was hooked. I was amazed - and still am - at the speed, skill and toughness of these guys. Sometimes, a player would run into the brick wall of three opposition players, you'd hear the crunch from the terraces and yet these guys would get up straight away and play the ball like nothing had happened.

This was a far cry from the overpaid prima donnas I saw playing professional football. I decided this was the sport for me, so I became a permanent fixture on the popular side at Knowsley Road, usually somewhere around the 40 metre to halfway mark. Old habits die hard - you can still find me there now.

In 1987, Saints reached Wembley to face Halifax and I was faced with a major dilemma, go to my first major final or revise for my German 'O' level oral exam, which was on Monday immediately after the final.

Needless to say, Saints won over the exam which, sadly, is more than Saints did at Wembley. I remember that day vividly, all the colours of the different fans, the noise of hooters and songs, chants and friendly banter between supporters from all clubs. This last point was what amazed me most. All this was not long after Heysel, when the reputation of British football and, by extension, British sport generally was at an all-time low. Yet here were 91,267 people mixing, drinking and laughing together. I'm happy to say that, despite many changes in the sport over the years, this has stayed the same.

I remember standing on the terraces, as this was before Wembley became an all-seater, while the pre-match entertainment took place. Leading the community singing was none other than Mr Womble himself, Bernard Cribbins. Of course, with it being a Roses final, there were Lancashire versus Yorkshire singing contests, with familiar local songs, such as *She's a lassie from Lancashire* and *On Ilkley Moor Baht 'at*.

From the game itself, I can remember only flashes, mainly because most of the people in front were much taller than me and so my view was obscured. I recall Saints freezing in the first half, before a Paul Loughlin-inspired fightback. I remember hugging and being hugged by complete strangers as Mark Elia went in for what we thought must surely be the winning try - only for that delight to turn to agony as we realised that John Pendlebury had saved the day for Halifax with an incredible last-ditch tackle. I can remember screaming for Wilf George's try to be disallowed, because I thought he was clearly in touch. It's not sour grapes, but I still say he was to this day.

Sadly, despite going to Wembley in 1989, 1991 and 1993 (my first non-Saints final), I had to wait another nine years to witness Saints lifting a major trophy in person.

Eventually though, happier times arrived. In 1996 Saints won the double of league and cup. By this time, I had moved to South Wales, so my opportunities to watch rugby league were limited, and my main connection was through Sky Sports' weekly live matches and the internet.

Now, I'm not a betting man, but I can remember at the start of the season saying to a friend: "I fancy Saints to win the title this year". I had nothing to base this on, although we'd recently signed Paul Newlove for a world-record transfer fee, and brought in a new coach, but equally we'd had a pretty poor Centenary Season, so our form was not good. Yet my prediction was to come true, if only I'd had the guts to put my money where my mouth was.

Anyway, when the title went down to the last match of the season, I decided I had to be there. Although I'd only been able to get to three matches that season, I didn't feel like a glory hunter, after all, I'd waited a long time for this moment! I bought my tickets when disaster struck. My parents, who were still living in St Helens, decided to visit that weekend. This called for drastic action. My parents came down on the Friday night. On the Saturday, I drove back to St Helens, leaving my parents in my house, watched the match on the Sunday, then drove back to South Wales the same evening. Everyone thought I was mad - driving over 350 miles in less than 24 hours just to watch a match - but that's what rugby league does to you. And you know what? I'd do it again!

Amusing memories

During one season of Super League, the club decided to make the entrance of the team onto the pitch a special event. So, just before they emerged, fireworks were set off.

Also Sprach Zarathustra was played over the loudspeakers and the players' tunnel was filled with smoke, from which the Saints team would emerge. Except, on one occasion things didn't quite go as planned. Sure, the fireworks went off, the music played and the smoke filled the tunnel, however, instead of the players, from the smoke emerged the solitary, small and spindly figure of... kit man Stan Wall. No disrespect to Stan, but it was a bit like expecting Goliath and getting Charlie Chaplin.

Anthony Sullivan plays rugby union

Normally I would rather have all my nails torn out than watch rugby union. However, on one occasion, I had a special reason. Cardiff RUFC where playing my local village side Cilfynydd in a cup match. The final score of something like 92-0 showed what an interesting game it was.

My reason for going was simple, the game marked the union debut of Saints player Anthony Sullivan, who was spending the winter with Cardiff. So, on a bitterly cold night, I trudged down to Cilfynydd's ground - basically just a playing field - in my Saints shirt. So he couldn't miss me, I even took off my coat, despite the fact the temperature was rapidly heading below zero. For about 65 minutes, he failed to notice me - then I was successful. As he walked back into the defensive line waiting for a kick-off following yet another Cardiff try, he looked at me, looked away, then did a hilarious double take, as he registered the fact that here was a Saints shirt in a small South Welsh village. The poor guy must have thought he was being stalked.

Keith Senior and the fish

One of my other recent memories comes from a Challenge Cup game. Barrie-Jon Mather had just scored a try for Castleford, when Keith Senior turned round and with a single punch decked Mather. I would not advocate violence in games, but it did give me a happy flashback to the early 1980s when mass brawls were a regular part of the spectacle. Later that afternoon, I bought a new tropical fish which, when introduced to the tank turned out to be quite aggressive - constantly chasing and attacking other fish. So, with memories of that afternoon's game still strong, I named it 'Keith'. I'm sure Mr Senior would be honoured if he knew, not everyone gets a fish named after them. I have to admit, it was perhaps a little unfair on Senior, the aggression he showed that day was very much out of character. However, it was such an impressive punch, I felt it should be remembered in some way.

Rugby league has given me so many memories over the years and, hopefully will continue to do so. I could list more: the time Shane Cooper hid the ball up his jumper to con the referee, or my personal favourite when Saints scored a try by heading the ball forward at the play-the-ball. The look of confusion on the faces of the linesmen and referee, as they tried to decide whether the try should be awarded or not was hilarious. Saints fans of a certain age will also remember the fairly regular spectacle of forward Roy Haggerty attempting a drop-goal. His style was often unorthodox: he'd drop the ball in front of him, then, usually about four or five seconds after the ball had hit the ground, vaguely swing his foot at it, and then look aggrieved when the referee called a knock-on.
These are all happy memories that will live on!

Gerard Bimson faced ridicule and humiliation from one of his teachers all because he watched rugby league. Below are his opinions and memories of rugby league and Saints.

Punished for watching rugby league

As a lifelong Saints fan, since 1946, I am risking life and limb, being burnt in hell and eternal damnation for even considering consorting with the enemy as the author of this book is from Wigan.

However, quite apart from my dedication to the Saints, I am also desperately anxious to see rugby league assume its rightful place in the British sporting spectrum. With that in mind, I applaud anyone who is making a positive effort to publicise the greatest game.

I have been a Saints fanatic since 1946 – apart from a couple of periods of enforced absence, the first due to National Service abroad in the RAF and the second due to a period away, studying for a university degree, I have graced the Knowsley Road terraces ever since.

But why did I start to follow the game? My connection with rugby league was cemented after a bizarre incident during my school days. I was still attending a local grammar school, where the only winter sport that was encouraged was, of course, rugby union, a game I played in a very average fashion for five or six years. I was not big and aggressive enough to be effective in the pack and was too slow and chubby to make a mark in the backs. For most of my union days I played as hooker and I remember getting really brassed off with the lack of ball-handling opportunities that came for the forwards.

This was the real 'kick and clap' era in union, with scrum-halves executing impressive swallow dive passes to fly-halves who promptly 'lashed' the ball into touch. Come to think of it, centres and wingers didn't see much of the ball either.

On one particular Saturday, I, and a few of my school friends had been playing in the usual inter-house union matches, after the game we were meandering down Dunriding Lane on our way home. We noticed crowds beginning to file in the Saints ground for the usual Saturday afternoon fixture. I had recently watched a couple of league matches and had been impressed with what I had seen. I then persuaded one of my friends to part with his pocket money and we both stopped off to watch the match.

As far as I remember, Saints were playing Wakefield Trinity; we both really enjoyed the game – forwards actually got to handle the ball which was great.

The following Monday morning, after assembly at school, our form master (who happened to be the man in charge of the school's first team) summoned my friend and me to the front of the classroom. He announced to the class that we had been seen attending the local league match at the weekend. For one minute, I naively thought he was going to discuss rugby league and what a good game we had watched. Instead he went into a theatrical rage and ranted about the danger of mixing with 'riff-raff' (his words) consorting with all sorts of dubious elements from the town. What made it worse was we had committed this offence while wearing our school uniform. He then whipped out a cane and gave us six strokes apiece on the hand and forbade us, or anyone else in the class to attend such a den of iniquity again.

Needless to say, I have been a dedicated rugby league and Saints fan ever since.

That particular incident has unfortunately always coloured my opinion about advocates of rugby union. Hopefully, times and attitudes have changed but I'm still slightly suspicious of their ulterior motives.

As for the nasty, dubious element among the crowd that our misguided form tutor was so concerned about, I can honestly say that over the past 60 years, the league fans I have met from every club in Lancashire, Yorkshire and Cumbria have turned out to be some of the kindest, most genuine, warm and friendly people you could ever meet.

I suppose you could say they occasionally get carried away with their pointed partisan chanting, and opposition and referee baiting – and initially that can be a bit daunting to a newcomer to the sport. In the long run, however, it's all part of that fantastic entertainment known as rugby league.

Going back to that period when I first became hooked on the sport, I can still remember the routine we schoolboys followed in the winter months. Friday night usually started with a visit to the local cinema – some blood and thunder epic, followed by a visit to the chippy on the way home. The proprietress, a big, cheery blonde lady, always had a blackboard perched precariously above the deep-fat frier with details of coach trips to Saints away matches on Saturday afternoons. As entranced 14-year-olds, we travelled to strange places with exotic names such as Wilderspool, Watersheddings, Thrum Hall, Barley Mow, Fartown and, of course, Central Park – it was absolute magic, thank heaven for big Laura's coaches.

For the first half of the following week, we discussed every kick, pass, tackle and knock-on from last week's match. Then from Wednesday night we discussed the forthcoming match. A few of us used to go up to the ground and watch the training sessions on a dimly lit pitch, which was usually frost-bound. Training, in those days seemed to be a few laps of a fog-bound pitch, followed by an intense session of 'tick-rugby' with some slick handling skills on show.

Because I have watched this fantastic game for years I have seen hundreds of star names. There were your own team's heroes of course and those you grudgingly admired in the opposition teams. Although the stars in the visiting teams got their fair share of barracking, their skill was always recognised.

I distinctly remember Brian Bevan swathed in bandages and looking malnourished, and this unlikely athlete ghosted from behind his own posts and ran the length of the field, beating every man in our team to plant the ball down under the posts. Not one player laid a finger on him. It was skill you had to admire, and every team had their quota of superstars. It is such a pity that these sporting greats never achieved the national status they truly deserved. Names such as Billy Boston, Tom van Vollenhoven, Alex Murphy, Brian Bevan and a host of others all deserve at least the same status and national recognition as contemporary icons like David Beckham and Jonny Wilkinson.

In our present game, names such as Andy Farrell (before his departure to union) and Paul Sculthorpe also deserve the same recognition.

The highlight of every league fan's career used to be their first visit to the Challenge Cup Final at Wembley. I first went in 1956 and even now the hairs on the back of my neck still rise as the final strains of *Abide With Me* die away and the match is about to kick off – absolutely fantastic.

In the Super League era, we have yet another superb showpiece occasion to savour and enjoy – the Grand Final at Old Trafford, another truly great sporting occasion not to be missed by any genuine sports fan.

We in rugby league should move heaven and earth to educate the country about the finer points of the game. Expansion is the key, beware of backward–looking, so-called rugby league fans who hide under the 'back to grassroots' mantle. This is no time for a fearful, chicken-hearted, approach to the game, we need to develop, spread the gospel, enter new markets and win new corporate sponsorship.

If we don't do this believe me, our union friends will, they already have the PR and media ammunition to do it. It is time to accept that rugby league is no longer an exclusively northern phenomenon and thank God for that. It's about time we shared the greatest game with others.

I hope this book goes some way to spreading the gospel and does not wallow in nostalgia. As fantastic as recollections of yesteryear are, it's time to move on. The only virtue in studying the past is to determine how to act in the future. It would be disastrous if we listened to some of the disconnected grassroots moaners and tried to turn the rugby league clock back to the 1930s.

Be proud of our heritage by all means, but understand that the way forward is expansion.

Ray Gent is a true die-hard fan of rugby league and his determination has seen him write three books on the game.

The fans' petition

Rugby league came into my life when the junior school that I attended in the 1960s allowed all the children one afternoon off to be able to go and watch Saints play Australia. Since my early induction I have never looked back and am now a home and away fan. It is simply a way of life. That first match was awesome and I was hooked for life.

My earliest memories include travelling by train to many grounds in Lancashire in the days when 'specials' were laid on. In those days the trains were made up of single carriages only with no connecting corridors. Travelling to Salford on the train involved being dropped off at Eccles with a walk of several miles to the ground and the Wigan, Leigh and Wire games also involved train travel.

Travelling into Yorkshire during the 1960s involved starting out at 8.00am on a Saturday morning for a 2.00pm kick-off. It was common to stop at a pub on the moors for dinner. There was no M62 then.

During a game at Castleford the local supporters pelted the great Alex Murphy with coins and as quick as a flash he turned round, smiled at the crowd and proceeded to pocket the money. Roy Mathias in later years used to sell watches, which sometimes saw him suddenly produce one during a game for someone in the crowd. "Any watches Roy?" apparently became a well-known saying in the crowd.

Visiting Rochdale at their old ground with its leaking stand roof was quite amusing but rather wet if you were in the wrong part. And I recall one part of the stand roof blowing off at Knowsley Road during a game and just missed a Warrington player. The match, of course, was abandoned.

On my first trip to Wembley we travelled by coach overnight, arriving at 6.00am. The gang all headed to Hyde Park's Speakers Corner where one of our number started to give a speech while we used our rattles in appreciation. In no time at all another 50 lost souls were standing round applauding him.

Rugby league books

In 2001 I started a petition about the poor coverage of rugby league in the media that attracted 30,000 signatures and was presented to Parliament. The petition travelled worldwide and attracted huge interest from many sources including Sky Television. From the petition a book was penned called *Rugby League Fans Say "Enough is Enough"* and was a huge success in rugby league circles.

The next book *Rugby League Fanpower - For the love of League* included the latter end of the story, including the petition being taken to parliament and then lots of tales about how fans help their sport in different ways.

The guest writers included David Hinchliffe MP, Richard Lewis the RFL's chief executive, Stuart Duffy of Bradford Bulls, Niel Wood, Stuart Cummings, Hull FC's player Jason Smith, Phil Hodgson of *League Weekly*, Gareth Roberts of sponsor Carlsberg Tetley and Peter Smith from the *Yorkshire Evening Post* plus, of course, many rugby league fans. This book sold out its print run of 1,200 in three months.

The third book, published in August 2004, was called *Rugby League in its own words* and is a possible first in sport in that it is written as an autobiography penned by rugby league itself. My co-author has been Tim Wilkinson from Leeds who is a talented writer.

Ray is passionate about rugby league and has tried to get the game recognised worldwide at the highest level. People like Ray helped inspire this book.

Lee Connelly is a St Helens fan.

When I look back on my fondest memories I find that rugby league always played a part. I associate it with my family because for generations my family have stood home and away at numerous grounds, some of which no longer exist.

My grandparents, both my parents, my partner, myself and my two sons have all shared memories of countless games and still stand in the same spot my great-grandad stood nearly 60 years ago. There are so many life lessons to be learned from our game which I instil in the children we coach now, such as acceptance, hard work, depending on and trusting other people, teamwork, unselfishness and respect for other people. But most of all there is the safe family atmosphere which has allowed our four generations to grow together watching this great game.

As a Saints fan I have many great memories, my favourite being when Matty Elliott collapsed in disbelief when Chris Joynt scored 'that' try, probably the best in Super League, against his Bradford Bulls in the play-offs at Knowsley Road.

I also recall one incident in a game around 1989 or 1990 when a fight broke out in a scrum as Shane Cooper broke on the blind side. He then sprinted the full length of the field touched down and turned round to see the ref and his touch judges trying to stop the brawl. Calmly he placed the ball and proceeded to kick the conversion.

Another moment in 1996 which sticks in the memory is when Bobbie Goulding was at Saints and was running the show. A fan ran onto the field as he lined up a conversion and knelt down in front of him and started to bow. He was led back to the stands.

Bobbie kicked the goal and went over to the main stand and knelt and bowed to us returning the compliment

In the 1987 Saints versus Wigan Boxing Day clash at Central Park, our arch rivals stormed to a 22-6 half time lead and it seemed there would be no comeback. Yet coach Alex Murphy turned Saints around with one of his famed half-time talks. We scored 30 unanswered points in the second half to win. Murph then led the team in a conga in front of the Saints fans.

I think my story is quite an interesting one because I am born and bred in East London.

My dad is from St Helens but I never really had much contact with him. I remember he took me to the Challenge Cup Final against the Bradford Bulls in 1997, and I just recall what an incredible atmosphere it was.

I guess rugby league is in my veins. My dad's cousin is Mick Burke the former Widnes great full-back. I went to see Saints twice more with my dad, this time at Knowsley Road and my love of the game has been growing ever since.

I even played for a while until my knee got mashed up. So an armchair fan I'll remain I guess.

Angela Cahill looks forward to St Helens playing Warrington.

I am originally from Liverpool and am an avid Liverpool football supporter. I went everywhere when I was younger to follow them.

However, I lived up the road from Huyton's ground and my mum used to work in the rugby club bar. She let me sneak in to watch their games sometimes and as rough as it was in standard it got me interested. From that time the only player I can remember is Geoff Fletcher.

When I got into my teens I met a Saints supporter and started following them in 1982. I have followed them ever since and have had several trips to Wembley and Old Trafford for big games.

I eventually divorced and in 1998 married husband number 2, Martyn, a Warrington supporter. We try to be amicable and it's not so bad when Warrington's results don't really affect Saints so I can afford to be gracious.

However, things reached their lowest a few weeks into the 2005 season when Saints scored right at the death at the Halliwell Jones Stadium. Martyn was in his usual seat in the stands and I was in the ground with the Saints fans. It was fantastic for me but my hubby was devastated and sulked all the way through a curry afterwards. Still we manage to keep it amicable - made all the more difficult sometimes as he also supports Everton - a mixed marriage if ever there was one.

13. Swinton Lions

Ian Jackson bravely risked being a social outcast when he decided football was not the greatest game on earth and fell in love with the undisputed champion of sports – rugby league.

Living in Manchester, you either supported City or United – and following a lowly rugby team called Swinton was unheard of – here is Ian's story telling why his heart remains true to rugby league.

I have been a Swinton RLFC supporter since I was a young boy. I have followed Swinton home and away since a fateful day at Station Road and an ordinary league game against Rochdale Hornets in April 1980. The moment the final hooter went I knew I would be watching the Lions for as long as I could – it was a weird feeling.

I was born in Manchester during the 1960s when both City and United were winning Football League Championships. However, my first two sporting memories are of the Belle Vue speedway track and the mud of Swinton rugby league.

Sport in the Manchester area was experiencing a golden period and yet it was only rugby league that uniquely captured my imagination and defined the way I would follow sport. Rugby league is the ultimate team sport, 13 players have to defend and attack as a single, cohesive unit and yet there is still scope for skill and individual brilliance.

And so Swinton RLFC is the team I support, and just as important to me, rugby league is the game of my choice. It defines where I am from, the social class I belong to, and has given me many hours of entertainment as a player and supporter.

Since these far off days of back-to-back Rugby League Championships in the early 1960s, Swinton RLFC has gone through some tough times. Players such as Ken Gowers, Alan Buckley, Johnny Stopford and Albert Blan are as familiar to many Swinton supporters as the players who wore the famous royal blue and white shirts of only a season or two back.

Exiled in Bury, briefly in Kendal and now in Whitefield has not helped the club's cause in the years since its traditional Station Road ground closed. However, during this period Swinton formed the first professional Supporters' Trust in rugby league and one day, who knows, we may be back in the Borough of Swinton and Pendlebury.

Until we do return home, the best game will always be the next one, as survival is the nature of Swinton. We have a long tradition - the Lions were formed in 1866 - and hopefully we have a long future ahead of us too.

My two sons follow Swinton now as well. Thomas, 10, and George, 6, help with the scoreboard at home games and then do what most youngsters have done in the past, which is play rugby with other lads on the pitch as the Swinton players are warming down after a hard-fought match.

So there is no doubt that I made the right choice in supporting Swinton RLFC and following the greatest game. The game of the community for the community: Rugby League.

14. Warrington Wolves RLFC

Warrington are often seen as underachievers in rugby league. Every season they seem to sign great players, but fail to reach their full potential, which is a shame because the Wire faithful need success. Hopefully coach Paul Cullen is the man to do it.

During the 1980s they had some outstanding players, including Les Boyd, Des Drummond, Paul Cullen, Les Davidson, Steve Roach, Dave Lyon, Brian Johnson and captain fantastic Mike Gregory.

The bright colours of the home end and the constant singing and drumming of 'barmy army' made Wilderspool a mini fortress. But despite having players like Iestyn Harris, Paul Sculthorpe, Allan Langer, Andrew Gee, Lee Briers and Kevin Walters they never brought home much silverware for the fans to cheer.

Eventually they will have something to celebrate and, with a brand new stadium, success should be just around the corner.

Warrington fan Neil Cooper is a constant regular on popular rugby league website rlfans.com and outlines his love of the XIII-a-side game.

Wilderspool Memories

I have been watching Warrington regularly since New Year's Day 1988. The first match I saw was the day the Brian Bevan stand was opened.

I had played a curtain-raiser in the Miller Sevens competition for Bradshaw Lane CP School, as the kids do now we got to watch the main match. We sat in the seats under the snooker club. I cannot remember much about this game itself, but do remember running onto the pitch at the end of the game, finding myself next to the centre spot and wondering what to do next.

Soon I heard the booming voice of the school sports teacher Norman Harrison calling us all back and that was the end of my excursion onto the hallowed turf of Wilderspool. I went to a couple of games after that, but watching Warrington lost out to playing Sunday football until 1988.

A group of us from school had kept in touch and after a few pints on New Year's Eve we decided to go to Wilderspool the following day for the midday kick-off to see Wire play Wigan.

Armed with storming hangovers and Mars Bars we walked to the ground from Grapenhall and squeezed into a space just in front of the scoreboard to witness what became the infamous New Year's Day war between the two sides, where four players were sent off and two more sin binned. That was it, I was hooked. Since 1989 I have been a season ticket holder and have probably lived my dream of being a professional rugby player through watching.

Having a displaced cartilage in my knee prevented me from playing rugby from the age of 17 until I was 26. But since 1989 I have only missed three home matches, two due to scouting commitments and one due to my honeymoon. Since my first encounter with Wilderspool I have also been lucky enough to play in two touch rugby competitions there and also had the heartbreak of missing out on a Warrington Cup Final spot when I played for amateurs Burtonwood Bridge a couple of years ago. What a lonely place the dressing rooms were that night after I had been told I hadn't been picked.

The friendly banter between the fans makes the game a great draw to me. Only twice have I experienced anything but good fun with other fans. Even now at the age of 33, I get a buzz going to the matches. I now live in Colwyn Bay so I have an hour's drive to get to matches, but it's a small penalty for the rewards of watching rugby league.

I watch any rugby league game shown on television, but any rugby union games apart from the internationals I find are a turn off. I enjoy watching local rugby league teams play even if I don't know any of the players. The game is just great to be involved in.

My favourite match

The best game I have ever seen is the World Cup clash at Wilderspool in 1995: New Zealand versus Tonga. It was so nearly an upset but not quite and the Tongans were so gracious in defeat.

The 1990 Challenge Cup Final, Wigan versus Warrington, will also stay with me for ever. Even defeat for Warrington couldn't spoil the occasion and all the emotion I experienced in the homecoming.

Of matches not involving Warrington, the two Saints versus Bradford Challenge Cup Finals were both great games, especially the first one where Robbie Paul scored a hat-trick but still ended up on the losing side.

I have seen some great players grace the primrose and blue of Warrington, including Les Boyd, Phil Blake, Les Davidson, Steve Roach, Jonathan Davis, Allan Langer, Lee Briers, Danny Nutley and Tawera Nikau. The last named is an example to us all, what he has gone through in the past five years and he has still got a smile on his face. I have also had the privilege to see the likes of Paul Sculthorpe and Iestyn Harris at the start of their careers.

Long live the great game of rugby league.

Freelance journalist Gordon Brown now lives in Cumbria, but his love of the Wolves, or the Wire as they were known in the past has never left him.

Sixty years with the Wire

The first time I saw a rugby league match was when the professional game restarted after the end of the Second World War.

I was about 10 years old and my father, dressed in his Royal Air Force uniform, took me by the hand and said: "We are going for the bus to watch a rugby league match".

We lived just outside Warrington and it was inevitable that if we were going to watch rugby it would be at Wilderspool Stadium, home of Warrington Football Club, as the sign announced near the main entrance.

When we arrived at 1.00pm, there already seemed to be about 20,000 people in the ground. Yet the kick-off for this match against old foes Wigan was not until 3.00pm.

We managed to get in to watch all the stars of the day, such as Brian Bevan, who scored the Wire's only try of the game in an 11-3 defeat. I was also impressed with Wigan's Brian Nordgren.

There was a crowd of 27,500, and with excitement at fever pitch I was pressed up against the surrounding concrete wall at the front of the Fletcher Street end embankment.

The occasion was such that I was bitten by the rugby league bug which has remained with me for nearly 60 years.

The trips to Wilderspool became a habit – over Bridge Foot, along Wilderspool Causeway, over the level crossing which had a footbridge for when it was closed, passing the Norton Arms and the Grand Cinema and onto the ground.

Memories stay with you for life, like the 1950 Challenge Cup Final win over Widnes at Wembley. On their return the team went with the cup to the Warrington Amateur League Finals at Rylands Rec and I managed to join the queue to get all the players' autographs only for my little sister to scribble all over them when I got home.

I had already seen the team with skipper Harry Bath holding the cup aloft from an open-top bus as it went through Kingsway traffic lights on a tour of the town on the Monday after the Final.

Four years later we had another Challenge Cup triumph to cheer, but not until after a titanic tussle with Halifax, who held us to a 4-4 draw at Wembley before we won a terrific replay 8-4 in front of a world record attendance of 102,569 at Odsal.

Warrington also beat Halifax in that season's Championship Final at Maine Road, when I was fortunate to be among the 36,519 crowd. That was a three-trophy season, because we also won the Lancashire League. The Championship Final win compensated for the disappointment in the 1951 Final when Workington beat us 26-11 at Maine Road. I was told this horrible result by a cyclist who rode past me on his way back from the game.

There have been many other successes over the years, such as the 1974 Challenge Cup win over Featherstone Rovers, and also there have been some disappointments, but true born-and-bred Warringtonians will always have an affection for their home-town team.

It is an affection we have taken to the new ground on the opposite side of town and although the shout of "up the Wire" has now become "up the Wolves", the memories of the old days will never fade and the enthusiasm, we hope, will never wane.

Colin Perkin, from Tyldesley has been watching Warrington since the 1950s and outlines his thoughts on why rugby league is special to him.

Warrington in the 1950s

I was born on 12 March 1943, and during 1950 and 1951 I loved going to the cinema on a Saturday afternoon to see cowboy films, cartoons and the Three Stooges.

My grandfather asked me repeatedly on a Saturday afternoon to go to watch the Wire. I was never interested and really didn't want to miss the Saturday matinee. After weeks of pestering, my mother said: "Just go with him once, when he sees you don't like it he will leave you alone."

So in February 1952 we took the bus from Cadishead to Warrington, a distance of seven miles, to see Warrington play Featherstone in the second round of the Challenge Cup.

We stood in the paddock on the halfway line at Wilderspool. Grandad told me to look out for Warrington's right winger, number two Brian Bevan, because: "he is the greatest winger since Jackie Fish who played in the early 1900s." In fact, said grandad: "He might be better than Jackie Fish."

Just before kick-off the teams were announced and Warrington had dropped Harold 'Moggy' Palin, their international loose-forward. At this point Grandad told me: "I am not coming to Wilderspool again," which I thought was odd, considering all the pestering he had done to get me there.

Warrington won 18-6 after a close first half, with Bevan scoring three tries and Albert Johnson with one from the left wing. On the bus going home grandad said: "They will have to play a lot better than that to beat Wigan, and they had better bring back Palin."

I asked when the next game was and he told me it was next Saturday against Liverpool Stanley at home. Of course we went. Bevan scored two more tries, but unfortunately I left the wooden box I stood on, on the bus. Grandad gave me a right telling off, but before the next match he had made me another one. I never did return to the Saturday matinee at the cinema and have followed Warrington ever since.

In April, Warrington played Wigan in the Challenge Cup semi-final at Station Road, Swinton, but grandad would not take me because there was a large crowd expected at the match. When he saw my disappointment he also decided not to go himself and we listened to it on the radio. Warrington lost 3-2.

Later in the season he took me to see the Championship play-off semi-final, Warrington beat Leigh 15-9, and then the Championship Final at Maine Road when Warrington lost to Workington 26-11.

During the following seasons we went to all Warrington's home games, plus away games at Wigan, Widnes, St Helens, Leigh, Swinton and Salford. When Warrington were in Yorkshire or Cumbria, grandad would take me to watch matches such as Swinton versus Salford or Wigan against Leigh. We travelled to all the games on public transport. With myself and grandad came his friend Bert, who always bought me a quarter of humbugs before the match.

Once a year, as a special treat, my dad (who was not interested in sport) would take us to see Warrington play in Yorkshire, and we visited Halifax, Huddersfield, Castleford and Bramley in his car.

One memory which will last with me forever is the Challenge Cup semi-final in 1952-53, between Warrington and St Helens. Before the match grandad had said: "If we win Bert and I will take you to Wembley."

Ten minutes from time Warrington were winning 3-2, with Bevan having scored the Wire's try. Warrington were struggling and the Saints scrum-half George Langfield dropped a goal to give them a 4-3 lead [drop-goals were worth two points then], and then within a minute Saints scored a converted try to lead 9-3.

Tears streamed down my face and I couldn't stop crying with disappointment. Grandad turned on me growling: "If you can't stand being beaten then don't come again." Bert, who was a nice man, put his arm around me and said to grandad: "Don't take your frustrations out on the young 'un."

However the following season we did go to Wembley and to the replay at Odsal, when my dad got his car out again. We also went to the Championship Final at Maine Road, and again in 1955, when Warrington beat Oldham.

Grandad's last Warrington home game was against the Australians. He was 76 years old and he said the steep bridge over the railway at Wilderspool was "too much for him". However for another few years he still went by public transport to Swinton and Salford when the Wire played there, or there was another good game in prospect.

He was, like me, a Warrington fan, but first and foremost he was loved the game of rugby league. I have followed Warrington now for 53 years, only missing a handful of games each season. If Warrington are in Yorkshire or London I will go to Wigan, Leigh or Salford. I will always try see a good game, that's what makes this game great.

The players are fantastic. Rugby league must be one of the hardest games on earth, they give and take knocks without question, unlike footballers who roll over in agony at the slightest touch.

They are also very skilful with quick handling, kicking and tackling. The pressure applied when near an opponent's line lasts a lot longer than an attack in football. The change to summer has increased the speed of the game, making it better and better. The advent of Super League, with the National League Divisions One and Two has eliminated most mismatches. There is now always something to play for.

My only criticism of the modern game compared to when I started to follow the sport more than 50 years ago is that the outside backs are nowhere near as good at side-stepping, as the likes of Bevan, Billy Boston and Tom van Vollenhoven were. Nowadays they run at or around the defenders. I know the covering forwards are much faster now, but when do you see a winger take the ball on the touchline and with three or four sidesteps come infield heading for the uprights?

I am sorry to say that this has long since disappeared from the greatest game.

Lynn Horrabin has followed Warrington for 15 years.

I am an ardent Warrington fan and have been since I moved here from the south of England nearly 15 years ago.

It was my dream to go and watch Liverpool FC play and stand in the Kop end of the ground - that was until I saw my first game of rugby league. It was a Boxing Day match with the Wire taking on Wigan and everything was just so exciting from beginning to end.

I remember thinking how unsporting it was for the crowd to boo the away team when they ran onto the pitch, but soon came to realise that it's just friendly and expected.

I have followed the Wire - some would say through thin and thinner - home and away ever since and have gone to many major finals and all the Great Britain games - not bad for a southern softie. Football for me has now become a World Cup only event although I did get to Anfield, but that was to watch Wire versus Saints.

John Tempest only discovered rugby league when he was 21 years old.

My first link with rugby league was when I moved from Stafford to Warrington when I was 21 years old. I had played union at school and heard of league but never seen a game.

After living in Warrington for a couple of months I was asked to make up the numbers in a charity game between two rival pubs, which were the Brooklands and the Imperial. I didn't give a thought to which code would be played and got the shock of my life when I took the first carry after the kick-off and was subsequently flattened in the first tackle and laughed at as I put the ball down behind me expecting a forward to scoop it up and trample me on his way forward.

A knock-on was given and I received a quick telling-off from the team captain. I explained that if this was indeed rugby league, then I hadn't a clue what to do. I was taken from the field to watch and then put back on 10 minutes later. I was moved into the second row and had the hardest 65 minutes of my life. I then joined Latchford Albion where I played until the end of the 2002-03 season. Unfortunately, a motorcycle injury wrecked my left knee leaving me unable to run again at the youthful age of 38.

I now watch all Warrington games home and away, every televised game, and Latchford Albion open age matches home and away, the kids on a Sunday morning and the Warrington Senior Academy side. If I can squeeze it in I watch the odd Warrington under-18 game. Without doubt rugby league is the finest game in the world.

Sean Kelly has many memories of watching Warrington.

I started watching my beloved Warrington Wolves in around about 1970 when I was aged three, but my first real memories are from 1974 onwards.

My dad Jack was the gateman on the then new south stand and leisure complex at Wilderspool and the place was rocking with Alex Murphy at the helm and legends like Mike Nicholas, Parry Gordon and company in their pomp.

Every Wire fan of my age was awestruck by John Bevan though, the guy was brutally strong, fast and would undoubtedly excel in today's game. Martin Gleeson is a very similar player in my opinion.

In 1977 I was nine years old and was rushed to hospital with a burst appendix. When I came around the next day from a lengthy operation John Bevan was at the foot of my bed. The memory brings a tear to my eye now and speaks volumes for John's work in the community, the guy is an absolute hero.

The two lasting memories I have of Wire games are the 1986 Premiership Final at Elland Road, when we beat Halifax 38-10 and Wire's magnificent victory over Australia in 1978. It has been a roller-coaster ride watching Wire for 35 years but I have loved every minute supporting my team in the finest sport in the world.

Danny Wilson in action for Swinton against Blackpool
at Station Road. (Photo: Andrew Cudbertson)

Steve Snape in action for Swinton against Cardiff at Station Road
(Photo: Andrew Cudbertson)

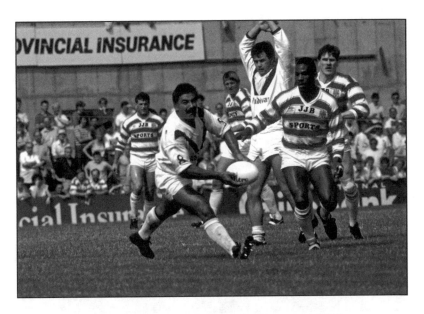

Kevin Tamati in action for Warrington against Wigan
(Photo: Andrew Cudbertson)

Warrington's Jonathan Davies evades the Sheffield Eagles defence.
(Photo: Andrew Cudbertson)

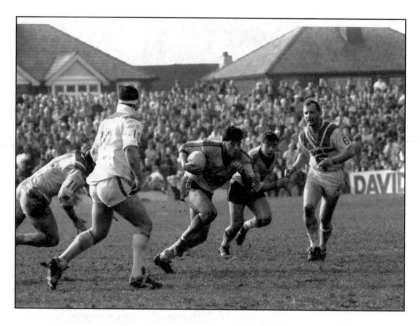

Widnes versus St Helens: Ritchie Eyres charges forward.
(Photo: Andrew Cudbertson)

Kurt Sorensen holds the Stones Bitter Trophy aloft to mark another
Widnes Championship triumph.
(Photo: Andrew Cudbertson)

15. Widnes Vikings

Going to the old Naughton Park as a Wigan fan in the 1980s was quite a daunting task, both sets of fans demanded respect and also demanded success, but there was always a bit of animosity.

Matters got worse when Widnes were refused entry into Super League, and for that they always laid the blame at the door of current Wigan chairman Maurice Lindsay.

They eventually got into Super League by beating Oldham in the Northern Ford Premiership Grand Final in 2001 and when Neil Kelly was in charge, they played attractive rugby and were hard to beat.

Before the Super League era began the Chemics were a dominant force in rugby league. With players like Martin Offiah, Jonathan Davies, Kurt Sorenson, Emosi Koloto, Andy Currier, Darren Wright, David and Paul Hulme they caused a lot of problems and won a few trophies along the way, including the World Club Championship at Old Trafford when they defeated the Australian champions Canberra Raiders.

It was in the late 1970s and early 1980s when Widnes really dominated rugby with outstanding talent such as Mal Aspey, Keith Elwell, Ray Dutton, Joe Lydon, Andy Gregory, Jim Mills and Mick Burke taking centre stage.

Jayne Greenhalgh outlines how she became involved with Widnes.

Naughton Park

I started watching Widnes when I was six years old, after my dad decided to take me to the old Naughton Park. Despite all the name changes the ground will always be Naughton Park in my mind.

Back in those days they had some fantastic players on show such as Kurt Sorenson, the Hulme brothers Paul and David, and the magnificent Jonathan Davies, just to name a few.

My favourite moment watching Widnes was a semi-final tie against Leeds at Wigan's Central Park ground in 1993. We won through to Wembley where we eventually lost to Wigan. What will stay in my mind forever is John Devereux's try in the corner and then Andy Currier scoring to put the icing on the cake and book our place in the final. I was only 11 years old and I will never forget it.

I suppose I am not so different to other rugby league fans, the majority are taken by their dad to try and relieve boredom and then you are automatically hooked and love every single game you attend.

David Basnett is a proud follower of Widnes. He is originally from Salford but has always supported the Chemics.

Widnes memories

My earliest and fondest memories of rugby league span over quite a few years.

I first went to a Challenge Cup semi-final at Swinton, it was Leeds versus Widnes in 1982. Leeds looked set to be going to the twin towers but late on Micky Adams's chip shot hit the middle of the cross bar, it was then caught by Kieron O'Loughlin, and he dived over to win the match. The Leeds fans were furious and were banging on car roofs with their fists after the game.

Another great memory is Jonathan Davies' league debut against Salford, normally the crowd would be around 7,500, but for this one 11,871 turned up. He didn't come on till late in the match. What I do remember is Martin Offiah scoring four tries, as if to say "If Davies is worth that much, how much am I worth?"

The World Club Challenge at Old Trafford when we beat Canberra Raiders in October 1989, a team which contained Australian captain and star Mal Meninga. The Raiders raced away to a 12-0 lead. The game looked dead and buried but the Chemics fought back to win 30-18.

During an international between France and Wales at Widnes, I remember the referee awarding a penalty to one team. An opponent continued to argue with the ref, who then kept walking forward another 10 yards each time. The ball went from one end of the field to the other all because a player would not keep his mouth shut.

One Sunday when Widnes had no game I went to Canal Street to watch Runcorn Highfield. On this day they finally won a game for the first time in years.

In 1979 Widnes played Wakefield at Wembley in the Challenge Cup Final. What sticks out in my mind, even though I was only a kid at the time, was the size of the Wembley steps - they were like mountains to me. After the match we were returning to the coach and I remember seeing hundreds and hundreds of coaches in the car park lined up in rows.

Another game which will always stick in my memory was a title decider between Widnes and Wigan on the last day of the 1988-89 season. We needed to win to keep hold of our title, Wigan started well but a Martin Offiah hat-trick saw us home - what a great day.

Keith Littler from Runcorn has attended every Challenge Cup Final since 1952, he now reveals his favourite memories about Widnes and rugby league in general, and all about his faithful push bike.

Challenge Cup Finals

I live in Runcorn, Cheshire which is more of a football town. We never played rugby at school so I never really had an interest in it. My father was from Widnes and took me to watch them play when I was 15 years old, back in 1948, and I have been supporting them and rugby league in general ever since. I am now 71 and have been to every Challenge Cup Final since the one in 1952 which featured Workington Town and Featherstone Rovers.

I was in the RAF at the time so I got weekend leave; I came home on the Friday, went to Wembley on the Saturday and returned back to camp on the Sunday.

Although I support Widnes, I will go anywhere to see a rugby league match. I recently went to Blackpool to watch Oldham versus Batley. In the 1950s I had a push bike and travelled to grounds, not just to see Widnes but any team.

Leigh was the first team to have floodlights, so when they had a night match I pedalled there and back, 20 miles each way. I remember one match I went to at Leigh. I arrived at the ground and stopped to get a programme. I noticed I had a puncture, the people who lived in the houses around the ground used to look after cyclists by putting their bikes in their back yards for three [old] pence. When I noticed the puncture it was only 15 minutes to kick-off, so I said to the house owner that I would mend it after the match. When I got back to the yard there was a bowl of water and my bike was upside down ready for me to take the tyre off. The kindness and help was much appreciated.

Another ground I used to ride to on my bike was Central Park at Wigan, which was another 20 miles. I went just to see the great Billy Boston play. In Wigan there were two railway stations opposite each other, I used to leave my bike at the station, go to the match then have my tea at British Home Stores, and then have a night out in the town.

The pubs closed at 10pm in those days and one evening when I got to the station it was all locked up, but I noticed a light in the station across the road. I knocked on the office door and a railway official came out. I told him my predicament, he told me not to worry because he had a key to the other station, and to my relief I got my bike. I had visions of walking round Wigan all night.

The first time I saw Widnes play at Wembley was in 1964 against Hull KR. After the match we went to a pub near Euston which had a piano and a mike. We had a great sing song with all the Hull KR supporters. We were even swapping scarves and hats with them. That's what makes rugby league so special, because of the supporters.

I once saw three matches in one day. I went to Liverpool City in the morning, Widnes in the afternoon and Leigh at night, all on my push bike.

In the late 1960s, I bought a car and I have been to every old ground in the league. Unfortunately, I had to give up driving eight years ago and my bike has long gone but I have so many good memories of my time in rugby league.

Pauline Condliffe was brought up in a footballing family so she found it hard to believe that her parents would go watch rugby league at the weekends, but as soon as she went as well she never looked back.

Discovering Widnes

I grew up on the doorstep of Tranmere Rovers FC and my dad worked for the Football Association, so football was predominant while I was growing up. I could explain the offside rule by the age of six, which is apparently not bad for a girl. The thought of watching any other sport, apart from the Olympic Games never entered my head.

I knew absolutely nothing about rugby league, I didn't know anyone who played it, anyone who watched it or anyone who wanted to... it just didn't figure in my life at all. But then...

When I was about nine my mum and dad started disappearing on a Sunday afternoon leaving me in the tender loving care of my older brother. I didn't notice at first because it only happened occasionally, but as time went by it started to become more frequent and eventually it was nearly every week, much to the disgust of my poor older brother. He didn't get any extra pocket money for putting up with me following him round on a Sunday afternoon.

Whenever I asked my mum where they had been she would say "We went to watch the rugby". Of course I thought she was lying, especially as the place they visited would change every week, Warrington, Wigan, Widnes, Runcorn Highfield - who? Not being a lover of geography and living on an insular peninsular of the Wirral I had never heard of these places. And why would she watch rugby when she could go round the corner and watch football at Tranmere like everyone else?

I was convinced she just didn't want me to know what they were doing and so I continued to ask her about it when she got home, confident in the knowledge that sooner or later she would slip up or just crack under the pressure and tell me the truth. But her story never changed, she was still insistent that they watched rugby league, although eventually it was only at Widnes.

When I was 11 years old, during the 1988-89 season, Widnes were playing Warrington at home in a cup match. It was a televised game, so it was on a Saturday. As I previously said my dad worked for the FA so Saturday was his 'busy day' (a bit like a priest at Christmas) so he couldn't go, and I don't know if it was because she wanted to prove me wrong and stop my doubting looks every Sunday tea-time or if she just wanted a bit of company in the car, but my mum asked me if I wanted to come. I had absolutely no desire to do so and even though I still didn't believe that was where we were going - or maybe it was because of that - I agreed.

By the end of the game I was cold, I was tired, I hadn't understood a single one of the rules, and yet I was hooked. Football - what's that? I just fell in love with everything to do with Widnes rugby league. The stadium that was falling apart, the funny accents people around me had, there was a smell of pies and stewed tea from the hut, and there were the biggest and scariest men I had ever seen...

I have been a devoted follower and season ticket holder through good times and bad since that day. I once asked my mum why she and my dad started watching rugby league in the first place, after all it was hardly the obvious thing to do for a woman from Liverpool and a bloke from Chester. She said "We thought it would be a fun thing to do, just the two of us, to have a break from you and your brother - I buggered that up when I asked you didn't I?"

Maureen Abbott has been involved in grassroots rugby in Widnes for a number of years, as a teacher of our great game. She gives a different outlook on rugby league.

Thirty years teaching in Widnes

I enjoy nothing more than singing from the rooftops the merits of our wonderful game, but for this book I thought that I would concentrate on something a little more specific - an area of rugby league that has affected me personally - the grassroots.

I spent most of my wonderfully happy 30-year teaching career in two schools in Widnes, where the grassroots ethos could not have been more in evidence.

It was the beginning of the 1960s and rugby league competitions were rife in the town with every junior and secondary school vying for numerous trophies. Wonderful days! St Michael's Junior School, and Saints John Fisher and Thomas More Secondary / Comprehensive Schools were hot beds for talented youngsters and became amazing conveyer belts for Widnes Rugby League Club and indeed Great Britain.

My first classes and ventures into teaching rugby, proved to be a piece of cake. With Mick Adams, (a future Great Britain captain) and little Keith Elwell (still in the *Guinness Book of Records* for playing 239 consecutive games) in my class it had to be.

Along with Reg Bowden (a future schoolboy town captain, Lancashire team captain and Widnes RLFC captain in the glorious cup-winning era of the 1970s), there was also Jimmy Nulty, John Myler and the most famous old boy, constantly visiting to present trophies – the great Vincent Karalius. For the then Miss Maureen Ryan, life was a peach.

In secondary school, life got even better on the rugby front, with more and more boys developing into major rugby league stars, and taking with them all the skills that they had learnt at school. I was privileged to be a part of it and there is no doubt that being personally involved at school level, brought enormous rewards for me. My most treasured memory (and my finest hour!) came in 1984, when the school was organising a Grand Reunion, and I was asked by the headmaster to research about all our rugby league old boys, as my contribution towards a huge exhibition of past pupils' achievements.

The task turned out to be overwhelming, but tremendously rewarding. I just did not realise how many boys had done so well in carving out amazing careers in rugby league.

One former schools captain of rugby had a large photograph hung in pride of place on the school's main corridor. The great Frank Myler must have been an inspiration to them all.

I discovered that in its 32-year history, Saints Fisher and More School had produced no fewer than 75 rugby league professionals, with 22 of them winning county and international honours. Along with Frank Myler, the internationals included Vince and Tony Karalius, George Nicholls, Keith Elwell, Doug Laughton, Denis and Jimmy O'Neil, Tony and John Myler, Colin Whitfield, Mick Adams, Dave Moran and Andy Currier.

The school produced no less than four Great Britain captains, and three of the old boys won the coveted Man of Steel Award: Doug Laughton, Mick Adams and George

Nicholls. We could only boast of one referee, but Robin Whitfield was an international. Beau Goulding (Bobbie's dad) and Derek Hammond (Karl's dad) made their professional mark through the portals of Saints Fisher and More, though not perhaps as dramatically as their sons.

Five boys became captain of Widnes Rugby League Club, and on one amazingly memorable occasion at Wembley in 1976, 11 of the players on the field were from Fisher and More High School. All were playing for Widnes except George Nicholls who was playing for St Helens. This is a feat I should think that never before or ever again will be equalled. Of course, I was there and no-one could have been prouder than me.

To say that these boys enhanced and coloured my perspective of rugby league is certainly an understatement, though I have to say that the power, the skill, the speed, the commitment, and the constant breathtaking bravery of the players had long captured my heart before I became a teacher. My pupils added enormous pride to the enjoyment of The Game.

Our wonderful game has given me and my family so much pleasure over so many years. Long may it reign, I love it, I love it, I love it.

Jane Naughton is a lifelong Widnes fan.

Being a Widnesian I thought I should write about my team.

I'm 41 now but from an early age Sunday was a rugby day, not a church day even though I'm a Catholic. A scrum down meant more to me than a sermon - no disrespect to church goers.

I would get money off my mum for the church collection basket but keep it for the game. My mum never knew and she is dead now, God love her.

When we were kids, me and my friends would climb over the wall at the snack bar end of the ground and get a hot dog with our church money - I did go to confession on Thursdays though.

My surname is Naughton and as a kid I thought Naughton Park was named after me so I had to be there.

I use to run on the pitch after every game to claim the players' tie ups. I got a good collection, I even got Glynn Shaw's headband, but every week I would come home disappointed because I never got Big Jim Mills' tie ups - he always said they were knotted.

But one week I went prepared: I took my scissors. When I ran on the pitch and he said his tie-ups were knotted, I produced my scissors and cut them off, how surprised was he? And how chuffed was I? He was my hero.

But nowadays in 2005 I don't have to run on the pitch, I can freely mingle with the past and present players as I work as a waitress at the Halton Stadium. I even get to serve my hero Big Jim his Sunday dinner, if only he knew that I was that small cheeky kid who cut off his tie-ups. Those were the days.

Billy Boston scoring for Wigan against Dewsbury at Central Park on
9 April 1960. (Photo: Courtesy Robert Gate)

Whitehaven versus St Helens, Challenge Cup in 2001.
(Photo: Peter Lush)

16. Wigan Warriors

Everyone knows how famous Wigan Rugby League Club are, fans either love them or hate them, it is as simple as that.

Since I began watching Wigan in 1986 I have seen many victories and memorable occasions involving Wigan, but obviously Wigan were a big force before the 1980s as well, with players like Jim Sullivan, Eric Ashton, Ernie Ashcroft, Billy Boston, Billy Blan, Joe Egan, Brian McTigue and Ken Gee.

Since I started watching I too have witnessed some great players, including Hanley, Edwards, Gill, Gregory, Kiss, Dermott, Platt, Hampson, Blake, Lydon, Offiah, Robinson and Goulding, not to mention more recent stars like Farrell, Radlinski, Newton, O'Connor and Renouf.

Mick Hannan, Community Development Officer at Wigan and former Under-21s and academy coach has a busy schedule with the Warriors and here he outlines his love of the club.

Central Park and much more

"You were only three, it was Wigan versus Warrington. We stood next to the hen pen. I sat you on the wall. I remember it like it was yesterday."

Those were the words of my uncle Joe. I wish I had a pound for every time I have heard uncle Joe and my relatives reminding me of my first time at Central Park. Born, baptised, first match – that's the tradition in Wigan. I know I can speak for many fans that have had the same experience with their own "uncle Joes".

In my spell at Wigan I have had the pleasure of meeting the stars of tomorrow, a bunch of lads that have realised their dream to play for Wigan. They are under no illusions that the road is long and hard and that the ladder has many rungs. If a few fall by the wayside it makes the others stronger. The ones who do not make the grade have given everything, sometimes too much.

The young modern professional has to give up so much at times that it becomes impossible to continue. They have to stay hungry to achieve their lifetime ambition to pull on the famous cherry and white and walk out of the tunnel in the first-team squad. Every young player has that dream. Let us hope that with the help they receive at the club they can achieve what they rightly deserve.

Like so many Wiganers who work at the club, you have to pinch yourself sometimes, brushing shoulders with the likes of Billy Boston who I idolised in my youth. Keith Mills is a loyal servant with dry wit that tells you he missed his way, George Unsworth is the kit man – salt of the earth (bath salts that is). He is the only man in Wigan who does more washing than any woman in the town and still has a 'dolly tub'. Brian Foley, the youth development manager, is so enthusiastic and committed to the development of rugby league and the future stars of the sport that he is a pleasure to work with. And I must not forget the administration staff who do a tremendous job behind the scenes.

Central Park played an important part in my life, as a supporter and an employee and I was upset to leave the ground. I recall my thoughts on the whole ordeal as we prepared for that final game against St Helens:

"The years may have rolled by and the old place has seen better days. The 'hen pen' no longer exists, but if you sit alone in the Boston stand as I do some evenings, you can hear the roar of the crowd, hear young boys asking complete strangers if they would get them through the 'hen pen' gate by saying they are dads, grandads or uncles. There is eerie silence but you can still hear the tannoy playing *March of the Gladiators*, see people hanging over the tunnel to see if they can catch a glimpse of their heroes, see Fred 'Punchy' Griffiths slotting over another goal, watch Colin Tyrer take ages kicking but being successful, the shock of hair on Bill Ashurst as he takes the ball to the line, hear Alex Murphy getting booed – "they only boo the good uns" says Uncle Joe.

I can still see Tony Rossi, Kerry Jones, John Ferguson, Shaun Edwards, Andy Gregory, Ellery Hanley and Henderson Gill – they are all there. I try and try to think about when I was three years old. Do you know I thought I saw Brian Nordgren and Harry Bath, perhaps it's because I have been reminded so many times about my first visit.

For the final game against St Helens, my guest for the day is my Uncle Joe, he took me to my first ever game at Central Park so I thought it was fitting to take him to the last ever game played there, and I won't let him forget it for the rest of his life."

Goodbye memories, old and new, goodbye Central Park old friend. Here's to the future in an arena fit for champions and to the spectators who deserve such comfort in a marvellous stadium. Enjoy the future.

Neil Davies follows Wigan home and away and is one for voicing his concerns after a bad display.

Home and away

I started compiling this after just coming back from my first away league game in London in August 2004. And we lost. Still, it's all part of being a supporter. I believe that you have to go through the bad times to really enjoy the good times.

I've just completed my first 10 years of attending games, during which I've been to every Super League ground along with several other grounds, and Wigan Rugby League Football Club has become one of the most important things in my life. It has become a standing joke at work that my boss just signs the holiday forms to enable me to get to all the games without argument, because he knows the grief he'll get from me if I miss a game. It has come to mean much more to me than just matches though, as I have also made some really great friends through attending games, and that is as important as the actual game on the field.

The first game I saw was the 1985 Challenge Cup Final between Wigan and Hull on television. I remember being mesmerised by two players in particular: John Ferguson and Henderson Gill. Shaun Edwards also played in that game, and he would become my favourite player in time, but on that day it was Ferguson and Gill who stood out for me.

Henderson's grin after scoring his famous try will live with most Wigan fans forever, and Ferguson just seemed to be everywhere that day. It is probably down to the fact that Wigan played in that game that I became a Wigan fan at all, and I sometimes shudder to think what may have happened to me if they hadn't played that day, given how important they are to me now.

Despite the profound effect that game had on me, I didn't become a fanatic immediately. After all, there are other things for an eight-year-old lad to do, and it never really crossed my mind to ask to go to a game during the following season. I did, however, start to keep an eye on Wigan's scores, and the Challenge Cup Final became an annual event on television in our house.

I didn't actually make it to a game until 1994, however, and that was almost an accident, or maybe an act of fate. My father was struggling to think of something to keep myself and my brother amused when he noticed that Wigan were playing St Helens at Central Park in a Premiership semi-final. I had been inside Central Park a couple of years before with my high school after Dean Bell and Shaun Wane visited my school for a term to teach rugby league as part of an agreement between the school and the club. After the term finished, the reward for the kids was a guided tour of Central Park, and this was when I got to meet my future hero, Shaun Edwards.

But in 1994, I finally made it to a game and became instantly hooked. It probably helped that it was against the old enemy which is always special, and that we won. My brother thought that it was ok, and dad seemed to enjoy it, but I just got into it straight away. I immediately made up my mind that I would start attending games the following season. I can't actually recall any real information from the game, other than the fact that we won and the atmosphere was great. Shaun must have had some sort of effect on that particular game, because for my following birthday I asked for a Wigan home shirt with his name and number on it.

The next season, I started attending most of the home matches, and my dad even started joining me. The season after I bought my first season ticket, and started to go to away games as well, my first one being at Headingley. By 1997, we were regulars at most games and have been ever since. My only regrets are that I became a fan just after all of our successes in the Challenge Cup, so I missed them all, and my first Challenge Cup Final was in 1998 when we lost to Sheffield Eagles. Also I missed out on seeing so many great players like Andy Gregory, Ellery Hanley, Andy Goodway, and most of my hero's career. Still, I have been able to see many great players and matches, and I've always got the videos to remind me of the past players.

My next big step was becoming involved with a group of Wigan supporters after being invited down to a training session, they were holding for a supporters' game against fans from St Helens arranged through an internet message board. I quickly found out that I'm not built for rugby, but this still led to me making some really great friends. I then joined the supporters' club and began standing with them at away games. Eventually, in 2003, I moved my season ticket over to sit with them all at home matches. This has made the games even more enjoyable, being able to have a laugh with my mates as well as watch the team.

There are many moments that stick out as memorable, both good and bad. The 2002 Challenge Cup Final will always stick out, not only for being the first time I saw Wigan win it, but also for the fact that it was against St Helens as well, and we were given no chance at all beforehand.

My favourite game so far though has to be the 1996 Premiership semi-final against Bradford at Central Park. We won 42-36, and Edwards scored four tries while still finding time to get sin-binned.

The last game at Central Park will always live with me, both as a good memory and a bad one. The atmosphere was incredible, but I wish we'd never had to leave, and I felt so deflated at the end of the game, even though we beat St Helens. However, as long as I can still see my team play, the memories will keep building up.

Jean Ellis has been watching Wigan for many years and even went to games with my mother before they both got married.

Central Park at night

I was taken to watch my first Wigan match at the age of 14 by friends of my mum and dad who were season ticket holders and fanatics. By the end of the game I was hooked. Then I started to go with the girls from school.

My best memories are of simply going to Central Park, especially for night matches, smelling the wintergreen, the lovely green, lush pitch and hearing the *March of the*

Gladiators being played. One thing I do recall from times past is only seeing a Wigan shirt in the crowd on rare occasions, usually won in a raffle. It was mainly scarves and hats we wore to show who we supported.

My dad told me that as a toddler in the late 1950s, I touched the Challenge Cup. It was in Westhoughton, where Billy Mitchell, groundsman at Wigan for a long time lived, and brought the cup to show the people of the town, so I was always meant to be a rugby league supporter.

Why do I support Wigan? My mum's family came from Standish and Appley Bridge so we were always from the Wigan area. I can't imagine supporting anyone else.

Jack, my husband, is a recent convert to the game and only started watching rugby after we met. I took him once and he recalls listening to what people shouted. One guy shouted to our players: "break his [an opponent's] black legs" and in his next breath was: "Come on Henderson Gill" (one of Wigan's black players). That was one of Jack's favourites, it was so ludicrous.

I liked Central Park, it seemed somehow a better atmosphere, the JJB is a bit clinical, too modern sometimes. And of the players, Stuart Wright will always be one of my favourites.

Most rugby league fans would do anything to see their team take on their hated rivals and Chris Mapp is no different– she wanted to see Wigan play Saints so badly she couldn't wait for a gate to be opened and ended up climbing over the turnstiles when she was pregnant.

Fifty years with Wigan

I have watched Wigan since I was four years old and I am now 56. When I was young my dad would have to take me with him and his friends, otherwise my mum wouldn't be happy. I have enjoyed many memories at Central Park.

Once I was late getting to a game against St Helens, the crowd was cheering and I couldn't get through the turnstiles as I was seven months pregnant. The stewards had to wait for someone to unlock the gate to allow me to get in, but I couldn't wait any longer. I then decided to climb over the turnstile – the man taking the tickets looked really worried, although I told him not to be. I couldn't wait any longer as I needed to see the game.

I successfully climbed over and we went on to beat the Saints. Two months later I had a lovely little girl called Lindsay. She too has gone on to watch Wigan with me and still does today. We have season tickets for the JJB as well as an executive room.

Lindsay worked as personal assistant to Sally Bolton when Sally was chief executive for 12 months a few years ago. It was like a dream come true when she landed the job – this was her team and her players. It gave her a deep insight into rugby league and the business side, but this did not diminish her love of Wigan RLFC.

We were there in 2005 when Leigh returned to Super League. It is so long since Wigan were relegated at Central Park. The year we went down, the Leigh fans sang "going down, going down" to us and we did. That was the first and last time I cried at a rugby match. So it was nice to have Leigh back at the JJB – bring them on. A memory like an elephant or what? Sorry, but that's how I feel, even after 25 years.

Below is my own account on what rugby league means to me, and how my love affair with the game began.

Sunday 28 September 1986: Wigan versus Hull FC

I was eight years old and playing outside with my next door neighbour, Andrew Taylor, when his dad Eric called him to say they were going out.

I didn't want to be left on my own so I asked where they were going. Eric told me they were going to Central Park to watch Wigan Rugby League Football Club, and did I want to go with them?

My parents said I could go, so off I went, really excited about watching my first game of rugby league, even though I didn't know much about the sport.

Wigan were playing Hull FC and won 34-7. I remember sitting in the Douglas Stand watching my new heroes in cherry and white score try after try on a glorious Sunday afternoon.

As soon as they kicked off I became fascinated with the speed of the game and the amount of skill the bigger forwards possessed. You could say I fell in love with Wigan the moment they ran on to the field.

The one moment of the game that truly sticks in my memory was when Dean Bell received the ball from a Hull restart, running 20 yards before offloading to Andy Goodway. Goodway sprinted 50 metres down the touchline and then sent prop Graeme West racing 30 yards to score in the corner.

I thought it was a fantastic try. It took me a while to realise that it wasn't common to see the Wigan number eight pounding down the wing to score. I think that is what made the try so special, because back then it was unusual to see prop forwards score from 10 yards, let alone 30.

When I got home, I wouldn't shut up about my new heroes: Shaun Edwards, Ellery Hanley, Henderson Gill, Ray Mordt, Dean Bell, Graeme West and one player who became my all-time hero – Nicky Kiss.

It was then that I found out that before my parents met, they both used to go to Central Park to watch Wigan in the 1960s and 1970s.

Due to my new-found enthusiasm for rugby league my mum and dad thought it was about time they started to go back. So that was it. Every time Wigan played, my mum and dad would take me and I have never once regretted it.

Because I watched Wigan through the late 1980s and early 1990s, it would be very difficult to pick out one outstanding memory, because those years were full of them.

However, one occasion is a little bit more special. It was my first Wembley Challenge Cup Final in 1988 against reigning Challenge Cup holders Halifax; the year that kick-started our eight consecutive final wins.

In 1988 Wembley was not an all-seater stadium and I remember standing behind the sticks in the Wigan end. My dad sat me on a crash barrier so I could get a better view.

The crowd was enormous. My try of the game was when full-back Joe Lydon raced more than 60 metres before sending Hanley in under the posts. In my opinion that was one of the best tries ever seen in a Challenge Cup Final, even though that accolade has seemingly been given to Martin Offiah for his try six years later against Leeds.

Even now in 2006 at the age of 28 I still get excited about going to watch Wigan. It is not the same atmosphere now that Central Park has gone, but my love for Wigan RLFC will never change.

I have managed to watch some of the greatest players in the world play for or against Wigan, including Hanley, Edwards, Andy Gregory, Mal Meninga, Wally Lewis, Brett Kenny, Peter Sterling, Garry Schofield, Gene Miles, Frano Botica, Paul Newlove, Paul Sculthorpe and the Paul brothers: Henry and Robbie.

In nearly 20 years of watching professional rugby league I have been spoilt for choice and the standard gets better every season.

Rugby league to me is the greatest game on earth; 80 minutes of non-stop breathtaking action, totally end-to-end stuff.

There are so many matches or moments I could write about but it is only fair to give other writers a chance. I know I haven't mentioned Wigan's victory over Manly in 1987, or the famous 27-0 win at Wembley against St Helens, or even the last ever game at Central Park. But over the years Wigan RLFC has made my dreams come true. I never made it as a player but the next best thing is watching, in my opinion, the greatest ever rugby league club – Wigan RLFC.

I just hope my son grows up and follows the sport we all love with the same enthusiasm and adulation as I do, regardless of who he supports.

This next piece is from a supporter who has had to put with my obsession of rugby league for years, my mum Kathleen Kuzio.

A family affair

I attended my first rugby match in April 1971, it was Wigan against Leigh at Central Park. Alex Murphy was player-coach at Leigh in those days.

I went with some friends from school and looking back I think I went out of curiosity because prior to then I don't think I had heard of rugby league. I suppose that isn't surprising as my dad was a Bolton Wanderers football fan and although I asked him many times he would never take me to a football match.

I went to several matches at Central Park over the next two seasons and then again between 1974-1976 with my husband, who is also a Wigan supporter. In fact when I first met him I asked him to take me to a football match. He did as I asked but took me to watch semi-professional Horwich RMI which was my local team.

I wasn't much impressed, preferring the rugby, and 31 years later I still haven't been to a 'proper' football match. If I ever did go and it was a no-score draw I'd want my money back.

Then in 1986 a neighbour took my eight-year-old son to watch Wigan at Central Park and from then on we hardly missed a game. We even got my side of the family interested in the game. My brother, who lives in Gerrards Cross in Buckinghamshire (diehard Wembley fans will know this is on the Chiltern railway line) went to his first match at Wembley Stadium in 1984. Unfortunately Wigan lost to Widnes, but that didn't put him off and he usually manages to catch a match when he comes to visit. More often than not it will be against Saints.

Speaking of Saints, it was the Saints versus Wigan Boxing Day and Good Friday spectaculars that finally got my football-mad dad interested in rugby. Between 1996 and 1998 he became an avid supporter. In fact he died on his way home from Wigan versus Leeds at Central Park on 21 August 1998; maybe he didn't like the score. Before realising rugby league was more entertaining my dad used to boast that he had never been to a rugby game and was actually proud of the fact, then he saw the error of his ways and was eventually buried in his Wigan shirt.

After that I couldn't face going to Central Park any more but every time I go to the Tesco store built on the site I say "hello dad" I vowed not to go to the JJB stadium because I thought we shouldn't leave Central Park but gradually we started to go and have now been bitten by the bug again.

On the last two Good Fridays my young nephew has been to the game with his mum and dad and during the 2005

Challenge Cup against Whitehaven, my son David took my grandson Ryan with him in the East Stand. I could see his little hands punch the air when Wigan scored.

And so it goes on. If Ryan becomes as fanatical about Wigan rugby as his parents are, they rarely miss a game home or away, he'll be a good supporter.

Simon Atherton is a very good friend of mine whom I have known for more than 20 years, all because of rugby league.

I first met Simon when we played for the same amateur team Ashton, before he left for pastures new. I then was reacquainted with him around 12 years ago when I decided to go and stand with the 'singers' situated near the Sullivan Bar at Central Park.

A life-long fan

I started watching Wigan rugby the same year I was born, 1977, mainly because my parents could not find a babysitter for me and my brother. Mum and dad were obsessed by the game, Wigan in particular, so me, my two brothers and two sisters all went to the rugby.

My first recollection of the great game came when I was about three years old, my dad would tell me about all these enormous men as we were travelling on the 610 bus to watch the game. My dad spoke so passionately about a guy called George Fairbairn who was later sold on to Hull Kingston Rovers, but I think most Wiganers would agree that he was the main reason we got back into the top flight in 1981, despite only getting promoted in second place behind York.

There was another player at Wigan at that time called David Stephenson who always took me by surprise by accepting a cigarette from someone would run on at half time. It is amazing how such a small thing can stick in someone's mind.

I recall two very frightening times at a game. One was at a game against Hull KR, we were sitting on the coach pulling away from Craven Park when a brick came through the window. My brother jumped on me to cover me. I was about five at the time and it was very cold on the way home. The other one was at Barrow. In the 1980s kids were allowed to stand on the pitch-side of the wall and Wigan scored a try in the top corner end of the ground, I couldn't see so I ran onto the pitch to see the try. There were no players around so at first I was ok. However, the players were on their way back for the kick-off and I was still on the pitch waving at my mum - when this voice said "hadn't you better go back now son." I turned around and it was dark, there stood in front of me was Barry Williams who was Wigan's full-back at the time. He seemed about 19 feet tall and built like a brick outhouse. Man did I leg it back to my parents who were in fits of laughter.

All of my fondest memories of watching the great game will always lie under the Tesco car park, which used to be the Sullivan Bar on the popular side at Central Park. The players I've seen and the matches I witnessed at that famous ground were unbelievable. The World Club Challenge victory over Manly in 1987 will always stay in my memory; I remember entering Central Park at 4.00pm just to get a good spot. I wasn't alone because around 15,000 more fans had the same idea – the problem was the game kicked off at 8.00pm. I am also lucky to have met some great friends all because of watching Wigan.

Playing rugby was also as amazing as watching. I left our home town club for pastures new, but I did score the first ever points for that team and I've got the bent nose to prove it. Rugby took over my life at a young age and long may it continue to do so. I love three things in this world: my wife, my family and the greatest game.

17. Workington Town

Les Brunton has been a follower of rugby league for nearly 60 years, being an avid supporter of Workington Town and taking in the odd Whitehaven game as well. He would be delighted if he had the chance to witness a top Cumbrian side riding high in Super League.

I saw my first game of rugby league almost 60 years ago when Workington Town joined the Rugby Football League in 1945, and have been an avid follower ever since. When Whitehaven were admitted three years later, Saturdays couldn't come fast enough - a game every week, either at the Recreation Ground or Borough Park, where Gus Risman was king.

My most vivid memory was getting off the train at Wigan as a 15-year-old schoolboy at the end of the 1950-51 season and seeing a large poster with the words: "'Ivison is the greatest ever', says Nordgren."

"Who is Nordgren?" asked my schoolmates? Well Brian Nordgren was a New Zealand player, playing for Wigan and he wrote a weekly rugby league article in the local paper.

The week previously he had seen Billy Ivison playing for Workington and beating Wigan 14-9 almost on his own at Central Park and thought he was the greatest rugby league player there had ever been.

Workington's defeat of Wigan in that final league game of the season had deprived Wigan of top place, and Workington were returning the following week to Central Park for the Championship semi-final. Before we went to the match my mates and I met an elderly gentleman in Wigan market who had followed Wigan all his life, he too said nobody had ever seen a player of Billy Ivison's ability at Central Park before.

He said the whole town had talked about nothing else for a week and how could Wigan stop him? I remember him likening Wigan's position to that of the England cricket team of the 1930s and what they could do to stop Australian batsman Don Bradman, that's how the fear of Ivison was affecting the whole town. Well stop him they did - Ivison broke his jaw. He didn't appear in the second half yet Workington still beat Wigan 8-5 with 12 men.

Workington versus Warrington in the 1950s.
(Photo: Courtesy Robert Gate)

Of all the tries I have seen, the winning try scored that day by George 'Happy' Wilson is the one I remember best.

To me rugby league is the greatest game in the world and the weekends can't come fast enough, while watching Super League on television on *Sky Sports* is just great. And even now I still get to as many games as possible including the international matches.

May I just add that Mr Nordgren certainly knew what he was talking about. For me Ivison most certainly was the greatest ever without any shadow of a doubt.

Rugby League books from London League Publications Ltd

Maurice Bamford

Former Great Britain coach writes about his rugby league heroes.
Published in 2005,
£12.00 post free

Examination of the relationship between Rugby's two code from 1895 to today.
£12.00 post free

Biographies:

Neil Fox – Rugby League's greatest Points Scorer
by Robert Gate. £18.00 post free

Trevor Foster – A Rugby League Legend
By Simon Foster, Robert Gate & Peter Lush
£14.00 post free.

All prices are reduced from the cover price for readers of this book.

Order from London League Publications Ltd, PO Box 10441, London E14 8WR (Cheques payable to London League Publications Ltd). Credit card orders via our website: www.llpshp.co.uk